Regulatory Mechanisms of 5-hydroxytryptamine 2C and N-methyl-D-aspartate Receptors in Pilocarpine-Induced Temporal Lobe Epilepsy in Rats: Neuroprotective Effects of Water Hyssop

Lyubov

Regulatory Mechanisms of 5-hydroxytryptamine 2C and N-methyl-D-aspartate Receptors in Pilocarpine-Induced Temporal Lobe Epilepsy in Rats: Neuroprotective Effects of Water Hyssop

First Edition December 2024

Written by Lyubov

CONTENTS

MATERIALS AND METHODS

RESULTS

ABRREVIATIONS

5-CT	5-Carboxyamidotryptamine
5-HIAA	5-Hydroxy indole - 3 -acetic acid
5-HT	5-Hydroxy tryptamine
5-HTP	5-Hydroxytryptophan
AC	Adenylate cyclase
ACh	Acetylcholine
AChR	Acetylcholine receptor
AChE	Acetylcholine esterase
AD	Alzheimers disease
AEDs	Anti-epileptic drugs
AMPA	α-amino-3-hydroxy-5-methyl-4-isoxazolepropionic acid
ATP	Adenosine triphosphate
B_{max}	Maximal binding
BS	Brainstem
BZD	Benzodiazepine
CA	Cornu Ammonis
CB	Cerebellum
CC	Cerebral cortex
cAMP	Cylic adenosine monophosphate
cAPK	cAMP-dependent protein kinase
CBZ	Carbamazepine
cDNA	Complementary deoxy ribonucleic acid
cGMP	Cyclic guanosine monophosphate
CNS	Central Nervous System
CREB	cAMP regulatory element binding protein
CSF	Cerebrospinal fluid
CT	Crossing threshold
DA	Dopamine
DAG	Diacylglycerol

DBH	Dopamine β hydroxylase
DEPC	Di ethyl pyro carbonate
DH	Dentate hilus
DNA	Deoxy ribonucleic acid
DTT	Dithiothreitol
EAA	Excitatory amino acids
EC	Entorhinal Cortex
ECD	Electrochemical detector
EDTA	Ethylene diamine tetra acetic acid
EEG	Electroencephalogram
EPI	Epinephrine
ER	Endoplasmic reticulum
EPSCs	Excitatory postsynaptic current
GABA	Gamma amino butyric acid
GAD	Glutamic acid decarboxylase
GEPRS	Genetically epilepsy prone rats
GFAP	Glial fibrillary acidic protein
GFP	Green fluorescent protein
GLAST	Glutamate/aspartate transporter
GLT	Glutamate transporter
GLUR2	Glutamate Receptor-2
GPCR	G-protein-coupled receptors
Gq PRC	Gq Protein coupled receptors
GTP	Guanosine triphosphate
HPLC	High performance liquid chromatography
iGluRs	Ionotropic glutamate receptors
i.p.	Intraperitoneally
IPI	Initial Precipitating Injury
IP3	Inositol 1,4,5-triphosphate
KA	Kainate
K_d	Dissociation constant

Ki	Inhibitory coefficient
Km	Michaelis constant
LC	Locus coeruleus
LSD	Lysergic acid diethylamide
LTD	Long term depression
LTP	Long term potentiation
LTLE	Lateral temporal lobe epilepsy
MAO	Monoamine oxidase
mCPP	Meta-chlorophenylpiperazine
mGLU	Metabotropic Glutamate
(+) MK-801	(+)5-methyl-10,11-dihydro-5H-dibenzocyclohepten-5,10-imine maleate
MRI	Magnetic resonance imaging
mRNA	Messenger Ribonucleic acid
MTLE	Mesial temporal lobe epilepsy
NADH	Nicotinamide adenine dinucleotide, reduced form
NADPH	Nicotinamide adenine dinucleotide phosphate, reduced form
NE	Norepinephrine
NGF	Nerve growth factor
NMDA	N-methyl-D-aspartate
nNOS	Neuronal nitric oxide synthase
NOS	Nitric-oxide synthase
NPY	Neuropeptide Y
NSB	Non specific binding
p	Level of significance
PA	Passive avoidance
PBS	Phosphate buffered saline
PBST	Phosphate buffered saline Triton X- 100
pCREB	Phosphorylated cAMP regulatory element binding protein
PFC	Prefrontal cortex

Pi	Inorganic phosphate
PIP2	Phospatidyl 4,5-bisphosphate
PKC	Protein kinase C
PKG	Protein kinase G
PLC	Phospolipase C
PQ	Panax quinquefolium
PWE	People live with epilepsy
RT-PCR	Reverse-transcription-polymerase chain reaction
RyR	Ryanodine receptors
sGC	Soluble guanylyl cyclase
SE	Status Epilepticus
S.E.M	Standard error of mean
SMOCCs	Second messenger operated calcium channels
SRS	Spontaneous recurrent seizures
SRMS	Spontaneous recurrent motor seizures
SSRIs	Serotonin reuptake inhibitors
SSRLs	Selective serotonin reuptake inhibitors
SUDEP	Sudden unexpected death in epilepsy patient
TFMPP	Trifluoromethylphenylpiperazine monohydrochloride
TLE	Temporal lobe epilepsy
VPA	Valproate
VICCs	Voltage insensitive calcium channels
V_{max}	Maximal velocity
VOCC	Voltage sensitive calcium channels
VTA	Ventral tegminal area
α2-AR	α2 Adrenergic receptor

Literature Review

Definition of Epilepsy

Epilepsy is a chronic disorder characterized by recurrent seizures, which may vary from a brief lapse of attention or muscle jerks, to severe and prolonged convulsions. The seizures are caused by sudden, usually brief, excessive electrical discharges in a group of brain cells (neurons). A seizure is a convulsive episode, which starts of as atypical, excessive hyper-synchronous discharges from an aggregate of neurons in the brain and then recruits surrounding neurons to comprise one or both hemispheres of the brain (Acharya *et al.*, 2008). During the seizure the person may experience the change or loss of consciousness, involuntary movements such as jerking, shaking or twitching.

Epidemiology of Epilepsy

Epilepsy is the commonest serious neurological condition affecting 0.5-1% of the population. Today, an estimated 50 million people live with epilepsy (PWE), 80% of whom in developing countries. Those most affected often do not come forward. Stigma, misconceptions and beliefs attached to this condition influence the open presentation of affected individuals in public meetings. The public health significance is particularly high in these settings because of its high prevalence, its seizure acuteness and frequency, and the sociological, psychosocial and financial consequences for the households it affects. Resource poor countries share demographic, sociological and economic features. They are particularly marked by ethnic, linguistic and religious richness, and their populations are frequently threatened by political instability and economic uncertainties. As a consequence health systems are typically weak and lack efficiency in addressing health needs (Quet *et al.*, 2008).

Etiology of Epilepsy

Epilepsy is often the result of an underlying brain disease. The most common etiologic factors of epilepsy that can predispose a person to epilepsy are head traumas, neoplasms, degenerative diseases, infections, metabolic diseases, ischemia and hemorrhages (Vinters *et al.*, 1993). In view of the fact that only a proportion of people who have a brain disease experience seizures as a symptom of that disease, it is suspected that those who do have such symptomatic seizures are more vulnerable due to biochemical/neurotransmitter reasons. The underlying cause may be structural, including a brain injury such as a contusion, infection such as encephalitis, lack of oxygen to one part of the brain as occurs in a stroke, or a tumor. In some cases, there is a brain malformation that developed before birth. In other cases, the cause is a more generalized dysfunction of the brain that is not primarily structural, such as a genetic or metabolic disorder. In a large number of patients, the ultimate cause is not found at all, despite extensive testing.

Certain brain areas, i.e. temporal and frontal lobes are more susceptible to produce epileptic seizure activity than the other regions. However, there are also patients with unresolved etiology of epilepsy (Hauser, 1997). Etiology of epilepsy is also a factor in determining cognitive function and intellectual changes over time. The main distinction is between symptomatic epilepsy which has an identified cause such as stroke or cortical dysplasia and idiopathic epilepsy which has no identified cause other than genetic factors. Lennox *et al.*, (1942) recognized that cognitive function was twice as likely to deteriorate in the presence of a known cause of epilepsy even if the idiopathic group had more frequent seizures. Idiopathic epilepsy is a type of epilepsy whose causes have not been identified. In such cases, the theory most commonly accepted is that this epilepsy is the result of an imbalance of certain chemicals in the brain (especially neurotransmitters) causing them to have a low convulsive threshold. Children and adolescents are more likely to have epilepsy of unknown or genetic origin. The older the patient, the more likely it is that the cause is an underlying brain disease, such as a brain tumour or cerebrovascular disease, or is the result of head injury.

Trauma and brain infection can cause epilepsy at any age and as mentioned previously may account for a higher incidence of epilepsy in developing countries. For example, a common cause in Latin America is neurocysticercosis cysts on the brain caused by tapeworm infection, while in Africa, malaria and meningitis are common causes, and in India neurocysticercosis and tuberculosis often lead to epilepsy. Febrile illness of any kind can trigger seizures in young children. About 3% of children who have febrile convulsions go on to develop epilepsy in later life.

Mortality

Mortality data of PWE in developing countries are scarce. A recent effort in China to address this gap revealed that PWE had 3–4 times higher mortality than the general population (Ding *et al.*, 2006). Most probably is the epilepsy-associated mortality also elsewhere considerably elevated.

Classification of Epileptic Seizures

The International Classification of Epileptic Seizures (1981) recognizes two general categories of seizures based on the origin of the abnormal electrical discharge. Two broad categories of seizures are recognized, partial and generalized, with each category having different subtypes.

1) Partial seizures, referred to as focal or local seizures, originate in one location in the brain and then may or may not spread to other brain areas. Partial seizures are further subdivided into simple partial and complex partial. In simple partial seizures consciousness is preserved. In complex partial seizures there is an alteration in consciousness, the person does not recall having the seizure and may be very confused and fatigued in the aftermath. A partial seizure may also progress into a generalized motor seizure.

2) Generalized seizures, referred to as "grand mal" seizures, begin simultaneously in all areas of the brain. Consciousness is altered and the person may or may not show convulsions.

Other commonly used terms include ictal (of seizure itself) and interictal (between seizures). Convulsion implies ictal behaviour with vigorous motor activities. Status epilepticus denotes a very prolonged seizure or series of seizures occurring so frequently that full recovery of brain function does not occur interictally.

Pilocarpine

Pilocarpine is a potent cholinergic agonist originally isolated from the leaflets of *Pilocarpus microphyllus* belonging to the Rutaceae family. It is commonly used in the treatment of acute glaucoma in humans (Hardman *et al.*, 1996). Systemic administration of pilocarpine has been used as an animal model for temporal lobe epilepsy and has several features in common with the human complex partial seizures. The most striking similarity was probably that pilocarpine produced marked changes in morphology, membrane properties and synaptic responses of hippocampal rat neurones, comparable to those observed in human epileptic hippocampal neurones (Isokawa & Mello, 1991). Single systemic high dose (300-400 mg/Kg) of pilocarpine injection as a novel animal model of TLE was established (Turski *et al.*, 1983). The systemic administration of this pilocarpine produced electroencephalographic and behavioural seizures, accompanied by widespread brain damage similar to that observed in autopsied brains of human epileptics. These electroencephalographic findings indicate that one of the most sensitive structures to the convulsant effect of pilocarpine is the hippocampus, while other structures remain unaffected or only slightly affected at early time points following injection. Studies confirmed that the hippocampus is the earliest structure to be activated according to electroencephalogaphic recordings (Turski *et al.*, 1983, 1989). One of the main features of the pilocarpine model that makes it very relevant for comparison to the human epileptic condition is the reproducible occurrence of spontaneous recurrent seizures (SRS) in rats injected with pilocarpine following a delay or silent period of about 2 weeks (Turski *et al.*, 1983, 1989; Cavalheiro *et al.*, 1991; Mello *et al.*, 1993).

Spontaneity is one of the prominent signs of human epilepsy, therefore strengthening the clinical importance of this model (Turski *et al.*, 1983; Loscher & Schmidt, 1988). Pilocarpine seizures also provide an opportunity to study the involvement of the cholinergic system in the onset, propagation and pathological consequences of limbic seizures (Clifford *et al.*, 1987). Behaviourally, pilocarpine seizures resemble other models of limbic seizures beginning with facial automatisms, head nodding and progressing to forelimb clonus with rearing and falling (Clifford *et al.*, 1987). In terms of neuropathology, the cell damage that results from seizures was identical whether they are initiated with a high-dose pilocarpine injection or a lower dose of pilocarpine administered with lithium (Clifford *et al.*, 1987). Lithium-pilocarpine is an analogous model to pilocarpine injection alone, except that lithium in combination with pilocarpine has been reported to produce a 20-fold shift in the pilocarpine dose response curve for producing seizures (Clifford *et al.*, 1987) thereby permitting the use of a much lower dose of pilocarpine. In terms of cell damage reported at the light microscope level, pilocarpine-induced seizures consistently produce damage in the olfactory nucleus, pyriform cortex, entorhinal cortex, thalamus, amygdala, hippocampus, lateral septum, bed nucleus of stria terminalis, claustrum, substantia nigra and neocortex (Clifford *et al.*, 1987; Turski *et al.*, 1989; Turski *et al.*, 1983). In the hippocampus, the CA3 and CA1 regions are involved and damage has been noted to be greater in ventral as opposed to dorsal hippocampal regions. Interestingly, the highest cholinergic receptor densities are in CA1 and the dentate gyrus, while the region most consistently and severely damaged is CA3 (Clifford *et al.*, 1987). This clearly indicates that the spread of seizure activity beyond the initial focus must entail activation of non-cholinergic pathways. Electron microscopic studies indicate the cellular changes include swelling of dendrites, swelling or vacuolar condensation of neuronal cell bodies and marked dilatation of astroglial elements with relative sparing of axonal components (Clifford *et al.*, 1987). The neuropathology reported with the pilocarpine model is consistent with prolonged seizures produced by other means (Ben-Ari, 1985; Kapur *et al.*, 1989; Hajnal *et al.*, 1997). These findings support that pilocarpine SE model is useful in studying the molecular mechanisms of neuropathology and screening neuroprotectants following cholinergic agonist exposure (Tetz *et al.*, 2006).

Role of Neurotransmitters in Epilepsy
Epinephrine and Norepinephrine

The modifications of the seizure activity by the noradrenergic system were reported early (Chen *et al.*, 1954). Four major observations have supported an anticonvulsant role for norepinephrine (NE): (1) selective lesioning of noradrenergic neurons with 6-hydroxydopamine or DSP-4 increases seizure susceptibility to a variety of convulsant stimuli (Arnold *et al.*, 1973; Jerlicz *et al.*, 1978; Mason & Corcoran, 1979; Snead, 1987; Trottier *et al.*, 1988; Sullivan & Osorio, 1991; Mishra *et al.*, 1994) (2) direct stimulation of the locus coeruleus (LC), the major concentration of noradrenergic cell bodies in the CNS and the subsequent release of NE reduce CNS sensitivity to convulsant stimuli (Turski *et al.*, 1989) (3) genetically epilepsy-prone rats (GEPRs), a widely used animal model of epilepsy, have deficient presynaptic NE content, NE turnover, tyrosine hydroxylase levels, dopamine β-hydroxylase (DBH) levels and NE uptake (Jobe *et al.*, 1984; Dailey & Jobe, 1986;; Lauterborn & Ribak, 1989) (4) adrenergic agonists acting at the α_2 adrenoreceptor (α_2-AR) have anticonvulsant action (Baran *et al.*, 1985; Loscher & Czuczwar, 1987; Fletcher & Forster, 1988; Jackson *et al.*, 1991). α_2-AR is known to have a regulatory role in the sympathetic function (Das *et al.*, 2006). The lesioning studies i.e., chemical destruction of noradrenergic terminals, reduce the amount of NE release; this manipulation also reduces the release of other transmitters released with NE. The neuropeptides galanin and neuropeptide Y (NPY) and the neurotransmitter adenosine i.e., ATP, are released at noradrenergic terminals and have been shown to exert anticonvulsant effects against several convulsant stimuli (Murray *et al.*, 1985; Mazarati *et al.*, 1992, 1998; Dichter, 1994; Erickson *et al.*, 1996; Baraban *et al.*, 1997).

Dopamine

The mammalian prefrontal cortex (PFC) receives a substantial dopaminergic innervation from the midbrain ventral tegmental area (VTA) (Bjorklund & Lindvall 1984). Dopamine is an endogenous neuromodulator in the cerebral cortex and is believed to be important for normal brain processes (Bjorklund & Lindvall, 1984; Williams & Goldman-Rakic, 1995). There is strong evidence that alterations in dopamine function play a role in pathogenesis of a number of neuropsychiatric diseases including epilepsy (Starr, 1996). *In vivo* studies have shown that dopamine increase and decrease spontaneous firing of neocortical neurons (Bunney & Aghajanian, 1976; Reader *et al.*, 1979; Ferron *et al.*, 1984; Bradshaw *et al.*, 1985; Sesack & Bunney, 1989; Bassant *et al.*, 1990; Yang & Mogenson, 1990; Thierry *et al.*, 1992; Pirot *et al.*, 1992). Dopamine favour long-lasting transitions of PFC neurons to a more excitable up state (Lewis & O'Donnell, 2000). *In vitro* electrophysiological experiments suggest that dopamine has multiple effects on PFC neurons. Both increases (Penit-Soria *et al.*, 1987; Yang & Seamans, 1996; Ceci *et al.*, 1999; Wang & O'Donnell, 2001; Gorelova & Yang, 2000; Henze *et al.*, 2002; Gonzalez-Burgos *et al.*, 2002; Tseng & O'Donnell, 2004) and decreases (Geijo-Barrientos & Pastore, 1995) in postsynaptic excitability of pyramidal neurons have been reported following DA D_1 receptor activation. In addition, changes in excitability mediated by DA D_2 receptors have been reported (Gulledge & Jaffe, 2001; Tseng & O'Donnell, 2004). The effects of dopamine on synaptic responses are also complex and species-specific. AMPA receptor mediated excitatory postsynaptic currents (EPSCs) in layer V pyramidal cells are depressed by a DA D_1 receptor–mediated effect of dopamine (Law- Tho *et al.*, 1994; Seamans *et al.*, 2001) whereas N-methyl-D-aspartate (NMDA) responses have been reported to be both enhanced (Seamans *et al.*, 2001) and depressed (Law-Tho *et al.*, 1994). EPSCs in layers II/III are enhanced by dopamine in rats (Gonzalez-Islas & Hablitz, 2003) but decreased in primates (Urban *et al.*, 2002). The cerebral cortex contains interconnected local and distant networks of excitatory and inhibitory neurons. Stability of activity in such networks depends on the balance between recurrent excitation and inhibition (Durstewitz *et al.*, 2000 ; Shu *et al.*, 2003).

A shift of the balance toward excitation leads to the generation of epileptiform activity. The presence of massive recurrent excitatory connections that depend on inhibition for regulation has been implicated in the susceptibility of the neocortex and the hippocampus to develop epileptiform activity and seizures (McCormick & Conteras, 2001). Modulatory influences strongly influence activity in thalamocortical (McCormick *et al.*, 1993; McCormick & Pape, 1990) and neocortical circuits (McCormick *et al.*, 1993). Dopamine is known to modulate epileptiform discharges both *in vivo* (Alam & Starr, 1993, 1994; George & Kulkarni, 1997) and *in vitro* (Alam & Starr 1993, 1994; Cepeda *et al.*, 1999; Siniscalchi *et al.*, 1997; Suppes *et al.*, 1985). *In vivo* studies in different models of epilepsy have suggested that dopamine may have a pro-convulsant effect mediated by DA D_1 receptors and an anti-convulsant effect *via* DA D_2 receptors (Starr, 1996). Dopamine-mediated recruitment of neurons in local excitatory circuits and synchronization of activity in these neurons underlie these effects of dopamine in neocortex. Local excitatory neocortical networks are complexes of interconnected pyramidal neurons. Several anti-epileptic drugs increase extracellular levels of dopamine DA and/or serotonin (5-HT) in brain areas involved in epileptogenesis (Smolders *et al.*, 1997). Behavioural and electrocorticographic studies in rats have shown that DA controls hippocampal excitability *via* opposing actions at DA D_1 and DA D_2 receptors (Bo *et al.*, 1995). Seizure enhancement is presumed to be a specific feature of D_1 receptor stimulation, whereas DA D_2 receptor stimulation is anticonvulsant (Alam & Starr, 1992, 1993). Decreased DA D_2 receptor binding in the brainstem were reported in other neurological diseases like diabetes (Shankar *et al.*, 2007).

GABA

γ-Aminobutyric acid (GABA) is the major inhibitory neurotransmitter in the CNS. It exerts an inhibitory action in all forebrain structures and plays a role in the physiopathogenesis of certain neurological conditions, including epilepsy. Impairment of GABA functions produces seizures, whereas enhancement results in an anticonvulsant effect. In tissue resected from patients with temporal lobe epilepsy, the number of GABA receptors are reduced in areas of hippocampus showing neuronal cell loss (McDonald *et al*, 1991; Johnson *et al*, 1992). Reduced benzodiazepine (BZD) binding to GABA, receptors in mesial temporal lobe of such patients can be detected *in vivo* by noninvasive positron emission tomography imaging (Savic *et al.*, 1988). These changes are likely secondary to cell loss and not specific for GABA-receptive cells. Recent studies have shown some changes in $GABA_A$ receptors that occur in the neocortex of patients undergoing epilepsy surgery. These patients had TLE with severe damage and sprouting in limbic structures.

Increased levels of steroid modulation of GABA, receptor ligand binding in neocortex were detected in patients with TLE. Increase in binding of diazepam-insensitive sites for the BZD ligand [^{3}H]Ro15-45 13 associated with the a4 GABA receptor subunit was also observed (Van Ness *et al*, 1995). Therefore, changes in the properties, rather than the number of GABA receptors possibly related to plastic changes in subunit combinations result in an altered regulation of inhibitory function. Human focal epilepsy occurs commonly in the mesial temporal lobe often associated with Ammon's horn sclerosis. This is accompanied by severe gliosis and a sprouting in the molecular layer of the dentate gym (Babb *et al.*, 1989) as well as a dispersion of the granule cell layer (Houser *et al.*, 1990). This loss of neurons in the hippocampal formation is evident in CA3 and hilus, especially hilar mossy cells as evidenced by several neuronal markers including glutamic acid decarboxylase (GAD) and GABA receptors. One can mimic these changes in animals by producing lesions or using massive stimulation of hippocampal input (Sloviter *et al.*, 1991), kindling paradigms (Cavazos *et al*, 1991), or systemic kainite (Cronin *et al.*, 1992) or pilocarpine (Cavalheiro *et al.*, 1991). Like the human condition, these models involve end-folium sclerosis, including hilar interneuron loss and dentate granule cell hyperexcitability. The granule cells normally are inhibited laterally by hilar intemeurons, which are excited by mossy cells that innervate them longitudinally. Loss of these mossy cells has been proposed to make the surviving GABAergic basket cells "dormant," thus disinhibiting long stretches of granule cells (Sloviter *et al.*, 1991). In the pilocarpine model, there is loss of hilar cells, including GABAergic interneurons accompanied by decreased levels of mRNA and immunoreactivity of the $GABA_A$ receptor a5 subunit in CA1/2 (Houser *et al.*, 1995). Loss of a5 and a2 mRNA was also observed by another group of investigators (Rice *et al.*, 1996) who demonstrated decreased GABA, synaptic activity in CA1. Therefore, in several of these animal models, there is evidence of reduced GABA-mediated inhibition.

Acetylcholine

The cholinergic system plays a crucial role in modulating cortical and in particular hippocampal functions including processes such as learning and memory (Ashe & Weimberger, 1991; Dunnett & Fibiger, 1993; Huerta & Lisman, 1993; Shen *et al.* 1994; Winkler *et al.*, 1995). Cholinergic actions are involved in the physiopathogenesis of epileptic discharges as suggested by the ability of some cholinergic agents to induce limbic seizures and histopathological changes resembling those seen in patients with temporal lobe epilepsy (Dickson & Alonso 1997; Liu *et al.* 1994; Nagao *et al.*, 1996; Turski *et al.*, 1989). Cholinergic stimulation of cortical neurons, including those located within the hippocampal formation, results in excitatory effects that are mediated mainly through the activation of muscarinic receptors (Krnjevic´ *et al*, 1993; McCormick *et al*, 1993).

Cholinergic innervation is present in the subiculum, which is a major synaptic relay station between the hippocampus proper and several limbic structures that are involved in cognitive processes (Amaral & Witter, 1989; Lopes da Silva *et al.*, 1990). Subicular neurons are also involved in the spread of seizure activity within the limbic system (Lothman *et al.*, 1991). To date little is known about the effects of cholinergic agents in the subiculum. The EC is known to be a "gateway" for the bi-directional passage of information in the neocortical hippocampalneocortical circuit (Van Hoesen, 1982; Witter *et al.*, 1989; Lopes da Silva *et al.*, 1990) *via* a cascade of cortico-cortical projections, the superficial layers of the EC (II and III) receive an extensive input from polymodal sensory cortices (Jones & Powell, 1970; Van Hoesen & Pandya, 1975; Amaral *et al.*, 1983; Deacon *et al.*, 1983; Room & Groenewegen, 1986; Insausti *et al.*, 1987; Reep *et al.*, 1987) that is then conveyed to the hippocampal formation via the perforant path (Steward & Scoville,1976). In turn, the hippocampal formation projects back on the deep layers of the Entorhinal Cortex (EC) which provide output paths that reciprocate the input channels (Swanson & Cowan, 1977; Swanson & Kohler, 1986; Insausti *et al.*, 1997). In addition, the deep layers of the EC also project massively on the EC superficial layers (Kohler, 1986) thereby closing an EC–hippocampal loop. Thus, by virtue of its extensive projection systems, the EC network acts powerfully in the generalization of temporal lobe seizures. The EC is also known to receive a profuse cholinergic input from the basal forebrain that terminates primarily in layers II and V (Lewis & Shute, 1967; Mellgren & Srebro, 1973; Milner *et al.*, 1983; Alonso & Kohler, 1984; Lysakowski *et al.*, 1989; Gaykema *et al.*, 1990), recisely those layers that gate the main hippocampal input and output. It is well known that the cholinergic system promotes cortical activation and the expression of normal population oscillatory dynamics. In the EC, *in vivo* electrophysiological studies have shown that the cholinergic theta rhythm is generated primarily by cells in layer II (Mitchell & Ranck, 1980; Alonso & Garcı´a-Austt, 1987a, b; Dickson *et al.*, 1995). In addition, *in vitro* studies have also shown that muscarinic receptor activation promotes the development of intrinsic oscillations in EC layer II neurons (Klink & Alonso, 1997). On the other hand, some evidence indicates that altered activity of the cholinergic system is relevant to epileptogenesis.

Serotonin synthesis and metabolism

Serotonin was initially discovered as a vasoconstrictor substance in blood and later in blood vessel walls, platelets and in enterochromafine cells of the gastrointestinal system, the lungs and the heart (Rapport *et al.*, 1948). Outside the CNS, 5-HT acts on autonomic smooth muscle cells, e.g. in blood vessels and the digestive tract (Zifa & Fillion, 1992). More than 50 years ago the chemical structure of 5-HT was identified and it was synthesised (Twarog & Page, 1953). Later, the function of 5-HT as a neurotransmitter in the CNS was proposed (Bogdanski *et al.*, 1956) and 5-HT has been studied intensively since its identification in the pituitary gland (Hyyppa & Wurtman, 1973). In the CNS, serotonin is a two step pathway from the essential amino-acid tryptophan. Serotonin is synthesised in the perikarya of the neuron where tryptophan is hydroxylated to the 5-HT precursor 5-hydroxytryptophan (5-HTP) which is then decarboxylated to 5-HT (Hamon *et al.*, 1982). To avoid immediate enzymatic oxidation to 5-hydroxy-indol acetic acid (5-HIAA) by monoamine oxidase (MAO), 5-HT is contained in neuronal vesicles until it is released into the synaptic cleft. Serotonin then activates either postsynaptic or presynaptic receptors or is reuptaken *via* the 5-HT transporters molecule into the neuron (Hamon *et al.*, 1982). The principle route of metabolism of 5-HT involves monoamine oxidase forming 5-Hydroxyindole acetic acid by a two step process. In addition to metabolism by MAO, a Na^+ dependent carrier mediated uptake process exists and is involved in terminating the action of 5-HT. The 5-HT transporters are localized in the outer membrane of serotonergic axon terminals and in the outer membrane of platelets. This uptake system is the only way that platelets acquire 5-HT since they do not have the enzymes required for synthesis of 5-HT. The degradation processes are very fast due to a large surplus of monoamine oxidase. Therefore, concentrations of 5-HT in cerebral extra cellular space and in peripheral plasma are low, and do not reflect serotonergic activity.

Anatomy of Serotonin System

The serotonin (5- Hydroxytryptamine; 5-HT) systems are widespread throughout the brain, with most of the cell bodies of serotonergic neurons located in the raphe nuclei of the midline brainstem (Palacios *et al.*, 1990). The largest collections of 5-HT neurons are in the dorsal and median raphe nuclei of the caudal midbrain (Jacobs & Azmitia 1992). The neurons of these nuclei project widely over the thalamus, hypothalamus, basal ganglia, basal forebrain, and the entire neocortex. Interestingly, these 5-HT neurons also provide a dense subependymal plexus throughout the lateral and third ventricles. Activation of this innervations result in 5-HT release into the cerebrospinal fluid (CSF), and measurement of 5-HT content in CSF in disease states will largely reflect this pool (Chan-Palay, 1976). This is another interesting aspect of the 5-HT neuron innervation of forebrain. Descarries *et al.*, (1975) has shown that the terminals of 5-HT neurons in forebrain, unlike terminals from other systems, only infrequently form synaptic complexes. Thus, when 5-HT neurons innervating forebrain are activated, 5-HT will be released into the extracellular fluid and its action will depend on the location of nearby 5-HT receptors. The organization of the ascending 5-HT neuron projections, the nature of their interaction with postsynaptic elements and the widespread distribution of 5-HT terminals in cortical and limbic areas indicate that these projections are most likely to be involved in the regulation of behavioural state and the modulation of more specific behaviours. The second 5-HT neuron system is comprised of 5-HT neurons in the pontine and medullary raphe with projections principally to brainstem, cerebellum and spinal cord. This system appears primarily to be involved in modulation of sensory input and motor control (Meltzer *et al.*, 1998). During brain development, 5-HT provides essential neurotrophic signal. 5-HT is known to play an important role in several physiological functions (Jackson & Paulose, 1999). Evidence from animal and human studies suggests that 5-HT is linked to many functions, such as mood, aggression, feeding, and sleep. Dysregulation of 5-HT function is believed to be involved in depression, impulsivity and suicide (Meltzer, 1998). Additionally, modulation of cholinergic neuronal activity by 5-HT plays a role in higher cognitive processes such as memory and learning (Altman *et al.*, 1990; Richter-Levin & Segal, 1990). Accordingly, alterations in serotonergic function accounts for behavioural disturbances commonly observed during epilepsy. There is conflicting evidence from animal studies, post mortem work and limited clinical trails as to the direction, magnitudes and significance of these findings.

Serotonin Receptors

The diverse effects of this neurotransmitter are related to the extensive projections of serotonergic neurons throughout the brain and the large number of distinct serotonin receptor subtypes. At least 14 distinct serotonin receptor subtypes are expressed in the mammalian CNS, each of which is assigned to one of seven families, 5-HT_1 to 5-HT_7. Serotonin receptors have been classified into families designated 5-HT_{1-7} on the basis of their molecular biological characteristics (Hoyer & Martin, 1997; Peroutka, 1994; Saudou & Hen, 1994). The $5\text{-HT}_{1B/D}$ receptors are found largely presynaptically, the 5-HT_{1A} receptor exists in both a presynaptic and postsynaptic form and the remaining receptor subtypes are expressed predominately postsynaptically with their distribution and density regulated with respect to individual brain area and functional state. Another protein important in serotonergic neurotransmission is the 5-HT transporter. This protein is localized on the membrane of 5-HT nerve terminals and is responsible for reuptake of released 5-HT into the terminals. The distribution of the 5-HT transporter conforms closely to the distribution of 5-HT nerve terminals (Dawson & Wamseley, 1983; Fuxe *et al.*, 1983) and thus serves as a marker for the integrity of serotonergic projections. The 5-HT_{1A} and 5-HT_{2A} receptors and the 5-HT reuptake site are the most frequently targeted sites of action for antidepressant medications and have been well-characterized physiologically. Thus, these sites have also been the focus of radiochemistry development. The 5-HT_2 sub-family of serotonin receptors is composed of three subtypes, the 5-HT_{2A}, 5-HT_{2B} and 5-HT_{2C} receptors. All three receptors are G-protein coupled to the activation of the phospholipase C functionally linked to phosphatidyl inositol (PI) hydrolysis and subsequent mobilization of intracellular calcium (Barnes & Sharp, 1999).

Classification of Serotonin receptors

The various effects of 5-HT on the central nervous system and peripheral organs are mediated through activation of multiple types of receptors (Hoyer & Martin, 1997). 5-HT receptors can be classified into seven classes from 5-HT_1 to 5-HT_7, based upon their pharmacological profiles, cDNA-deduced primary sequences and signal transduction mechanisms of receptors (Bradley *et al.*, 1986; Zifa & Fillion, 1992). All 5-HT receptors belong to the superfamily of G-protein coupled receptors containing a seven transmembrane domain structure except 5-HT_3 receptor, which forms a ligand-gated ion channel.

5-HT₁ Receptor

At least five 5-HT_1 receptor subtypes have been recognised, 5-HT_{1A}, 5-HT_{1B}, 5-HT_{1D}, 5-HT_{1E} and 5-HT_{1F}. All are seven transmembrane, G-protein coupled receptors *via* Gi or Go, encoded by intronless genes, between 365 and 422 amino acids with an overall sequence homology of 40%. 5-HT_{1A} receptor subtype which is located on human chromosome 5cenq11 is widely distributed in the CNS, particularly hippocampus (Hoyer *et al.*, 1994). The 5-HT$_{1B}$ receptor is located on human chromosome 6q13 and is concentrated in the basal ganglia, striatum and frontal cortex. The receptor is negatively coupled to adenylyl cyclase. The 5-HT$_{1D}$ receptor has 63% overall structural homology to 5-HT$_{1B}$ receptor and 77% amino acid sequence homology in the seven transmebrane domains. The receptor is located on human gene 1p36.3-p34.3 and is negatively linked to adenylyl cyclase. 5HT$_{1D}$ receptor mRNA is found in the rat brain, predominantly in the caudate putamen, nucleus accumbens, hippocampus, cortex, dorsal raphe and locus ceoruleus (Hoyer *et al.*, 1994). The 5-HT$_{1E}$ receptor was first characterised in man as a [^{3}H] 5-HT binding site in the presence of 5-carboxyamidotryptamine (5-CT) to block binding to the 5-HT$_{1A}$ and 5-HT$_{1D}$ receptors. Human brain binding studies have reported that 5-HT$_{1E}$ receptors are concentrated in the caudate putamen with lower levels in the amygdala, frontal cortex and globus pallidus. This is consistent with the observed distribution of 5-HT$_{1C}$ mRNA (Hoyer *et al.*, 1994). The receptor has been mapped to human chromosome 6q14-q15, is negatively linked to adenylyl cyclase and consists of a 365 amino acid protein with seven transmembrane domains. 5-HT$_{1F}$ receptor subtype is most closely related to the 5-HT$_{1E}$ receptor with 70% sequence homology across the 7 transmembrane domains. mRNA coding for the receptor is concentrated in the dorsal raphe, hippocampus and cortex of the rat and also in the striatum, thalamus and hypothalamus of the mouse (Hoyer *et al.*, 1994). The receptor is negatively linked to adenylyl cyclase.

5-HT$_2$ Receptor

The 5-HT$_2$ receptor family consists of three subtypes namely 5-HT$_{2A}$, 5-HT$_{2B}$ and 5-HT$_{2C}$. 5-HT$_{2C}$ was previously termed as 5-HT$_{1C}$ before its structural similarity to the 5-HT$_2$ family members was recognized. All three are single protein molecules of 458 - 471 amino acids with an overall homology of approximately 50% rising to between 70-80% in the seven transmembrane domains. All three are thought to be linked to the phosphoinositol hydrolysis signal transduction system *via* the α subunit of Gq protein. In human pulmonary artery endothelial cells, 5-HT$_{2C}$ receptor stimulation causes intracellular calcium release *via* a mechanism independent of phosphatidylinositol hydrolysis (Hagan *et al.*, 1995). 5-HT$_{2A}$ receptor previously termed as 5HT$_2$ receptor is located on human chromosome 13q14-q21 and is widely distributed in peripheral tissues. It mediates contractile responses of vascular, urinary, gastrointestinal and uterine smooth muscle preparations, platelet aggregation and increased capillary permeability in both rodent and human tissue (Hoyer *et al.*, 1994). The 5-HT$_{2B}$ receptor located on chromosome 2q36-2q37.1 mediates contraction of the rat stomach fundus and endothelium dependent relaxation of the rat and cat jugular veins and possibly of the pig pulmonary artery, *via* nitric oxide release (Choi & Maroteaux, 1996). 5-HT$_{2B}$ receptor mRNA has been detected throughout the mouse, rat and guinea pig colon and small intestine. 5-HT$_{2C}$ specific antibodies have recently used to show the presence of the receptor protein in the choroid plexus (highest density) and at a lower level in the cerebral cortex, hippocampus, striatum, and substantia nigra of rat and a similar distribution in man. The receptor has been mapped to human chromosome Xq24. No splice variants have been reported but the receptor is capable of post translational modification whereby adenosine residues can be represented as guanosine in the second loop to yield 4 variants.

5-HT$_3$ Receptor

The 5-HT$_3$ receptor binding site is widely distributed both centrally and peripherally and has been detected in a number of neuronally derived cells. The highest densities are found in the area postrema, nucleus tractus solitarius, substantia gelatinosa and nuclei of the lower brainstem. It is also found in higher brain areas such as the cortex, hippocampus, amygdala and medial habenula but at lower densities. Unlike other 5-HT receptors, 5-HT$_3$ receptor subunits form a pentameric cation channel that is selectively permeable to Na^+, K^+ and Ca^{++} ions causing depolarisation. The $5-HT_3$ receptor is a member of a superfamily of ligand-gated ion channels, which includes the muscle and neuronal nicotinic acetylcholine receptor (AChR), the glycine receptor, and the γ aminobutyric acid type A receptor (Karlin & Akabas, 1995; Ortells & Lunt, 1995). Like the other members of this gene superfamily, the $5HT_3$ receptor exhibits a large degree of sequence similarity and thus presumably structural homology with the AchR (Maricq *et al.*, 1991).

5-HT₄ Receptor

Receptor binding studies have established that the $5-HT_4$ receptor is highly concentrated in areas of the rat brain associated with dopamine function such as the striatum, basal ganglia and nucleus accumbens. These receptors are also located on GABAergic or cholinergic interneurons and/or on GABAergic projections to the substantia nigra (Patel *et al.*, 1995). The receptor is functionally coupled to the G protein.

5-HT₅ Receptor

Two 5-HT receptors identified from rat cDNA and cloned were found to have 88% overall sequence homology, yet were not closely related to any other 5-HT receptor family (Erlander *et al.*, 1993). These receptors have thus been classified as $5-HT_{5A}$ and $5-HT_{5B}$ and their mRNAs have been located in man (Grailhe *et al.*, 1994). In cells expressing the cloned rat $5-HT_{5A}$ site, the receptor was negatively linked to adenylyl cyclase and acts as terminal autoreceptors in the mouse frontal cortex (Wisden *et al.*, 1993).

5-HT₆ Receptor

Like the $5-HT_5$ receptor, the $5-HT_6$ receptor has been cloned from rat cDNA based on its homology to previously cloned G protein coupled receptors. The rat receptor consists of 438 amino acids with seven transmembrane domains and is positively coupled to adenylyl cyclase *via* the Gs G protein. The human gene has been cloned and has 89% sequence homology with its rat equivalent and is coupled to adenylyl cyclase (Kohen *et al.*, 1996). Rat and human $5-HT_6$ mRNA is located in the striatum, amygdala, nucleus accumbens, hippocampus, cortex and olfactory tubercle, but has not been found in peripheral organs studied (Kohen *et al.*, 1996).

5-HT₇ Receptor

$5-HT_7$ receptor has been cloned from rat, mouse, guinea pig and human cDNA and is located on human chromosome 10q23.3-q24.4. Despite a high degree of interspecies homology (95%) the receptor has low homology (<40%) with other 5-HT receptor subtypes. The human receptor has a sequence of 445 amino acids and appears to form a receptor with seven transmembrane domains.

$5-HT_{2C}$ Receptor Structure

The $5-HT_{2C}$ receptor was identified as a tritiated-5-HT binding site in the choroid plexus, tissue involved in production of CSF of various species that could also be labeled by tritiated-mesulergine and tritiated-lysergic acid diethylamide (LSD). Originally this site was seen as a new member of the $5-HT_1$ receptor family and termed $5-HT_{1C}$, because of its high affinity for $[^3H]5-HT$ (Pazos *et al.*, 1999). However, once the receptor was cloned and more information about its characteristics became available, a shift to the $5-HT_2$ receptor family and reclassification as $5-HT_{2C}$ receptors became accepted (Humphrey *et al.*, 1993). The partial cloning of the mouse $5-HT_{2C}$ receptor (Lubbert *et al.*, 1987) was shortly followed by the sequencing of the full length clone in the rat (Julius *et al.*, 1989), mouse (Yu *et al.*, 1991) and human (Saltzman *et al.*, 1991). Additionally, a splice variant of the $5-HT_{2C}$ receptor has been observed in brain tissues of the rat, mouse and human (Canton *et al.*, 1996). The functional significance of this variant is however, unclear as the protein product is truncated and lacks a 5-HT binding site. More recently, it has been reported that 5-HT$_{2C}$ mRNA undergoes post-transcriptional editing to yield multiple 5-HT$_{2C}$ receptor isoforms with different distributions in brain. In functional terms, this is potentially of great significance as the amino acid sequences predicted from the mRNA transcripts indicate that the isoforms if expressed endogenously in significant amounts in brain tissue have different regulatory and pharmacological properties (Burns *et al.*, 1997). The gene for the 5-HT$_{2C}$ receptor is located on the human X chromosome at position q 24 (Xq24). The 5-HT$_{2C}$ receptor gene has three introns rather than two as in the case of the 5-HT$_{2A}$ and 5-HT$_{2B}$ produce a protein product with eight rather than seven transmembrane regions, which, if proven, would be unusual for a G-protein coupled receptor (Yu *et al.*, 1991). There is high sequence homology, >80% in the transmembrane regions, between the mouse, rat and human 5-HT$_{2C}$ receptors. The mouse and rat 5-HT$_{2C}$ receptors possess six potential N-glycosylation sites, four of which are conserved in the human sequence. The rat 5-HT$_{2C}$ receptor has eight serine/threonine residues representing possible phosphorylation sites, all of which are conserved in the human sequence (Barnes & Sharp, 1999).

Functional Effects Mediated *via* the 5-HT$_{2C}$ Receptor Signal Transduction

Agonist binding to the 5-HT$_{2C}$ receptor activates phospholipase C *via* activation of a G protein (Gq11). Phospholipase C catalyzes the hydrolysis of phosphatidylinositol-4, 5-bisphosphate to inositol 1,4,5-triphosphate and diacylglycerol. Inositol 1,4,5-triphosphate, acting as a second messenger, diffuses through the cell cytoplasm and stimulates the release of calcium sequestered in the endoplasmic reticulum which in turn activates numerous cellular processes through the intermediacy of calmodulin and its homologs. The diacylglycerol remains associated with the plasma membrane where it activates protein kinase C to phosphorylate and thereby modulate the activities of a number of cellular proteins. It has been suggested that 5-HT$_{2C}$ receptors in choroid plexus may regulate CSF formation as a result of their ability mediate cyclic guanosine monophosphate (cGMP) formation (Schlunzen *et al.*, 1988; Boess & Martin, 1994; Conn *et al.*, 1987; Kaufman *et al.*, 1995).

Genetic and molecular events regulate the creation of variants of 5-HT$_{2A}$ and 5-HT$_{2C}$ receptors whose diversity has important functional significance. Overall sequence identity between the 5-HT$_{2A}$ and 5-HT$_{2C}$ receptors is quite high and it is not surprising that the mechanisms of regulation for these two receptors are similar. There is, however, one striking difference between these two receptors, which involves RNA editing a mechanism for generating molecular diversity by altering the genetic code at the level of RNA. The 5-HT$_{2C}$ receptor is the only known G protein-coupled receptor whose mRNA undergoes post-transcriptional editing to yield different receptor isoforms (Sander-Bush *et al.*, 2003). The different 5-HT$_{2C}$ receptor isoforms generated from RNA editing have demonstrated altered dynamics of agonist-induced calcium release. These distinctions in agonist-induced calcium release imply that edited 5-HT$_{2C}$ receptors may produce distinct physiological responses within the CNS (Price & Sanders-Bush, 2000). It has been shown that editing sites are located on the second intracellular loop, which contains a consensus sequence for G-protein interaction (Niswender *et al.*, 1999). It is therefore clear that changes in amino acid sequence affect the coupling ability between the receptor and its protein. In this regard, it was recently reported that depletion of serotonin increases expression of 5-HT$_{2C}$ mRNA isoforms encoding receptors with higher sensitivity to serotonin. These results indicate that mRNA editing serves as a mechanism whereby 5-HT$_{2C}$ receptor activity is stabilized in the face of changing synaptic serotonergic input (Gurevich *et al.*, 2002).

Serotonin and Serotonin Receptors in Epilepsy

The general recognition that serotonin plays a role in epileptic mechanisms is based on several lines of evidence from studies in both animal models of epilepsy and humans. In the genetically epilepsy-prone rat (GEPR) model of generalized epilepsy, a decrease is found in brain concentration of serotonin (Dailey *et al.*, 1989) as well as decreased V_{max} for $[^3H]$ serotonin uptake by synaptosomes and tryptophan hydroxylase activity (Statnick *et al.*, 1996). Pharmacologic treatments that facilitate serotonergic neurotransmission inhibit seizures in many animal models of epilepsy, including the GEPR rat, maximal electroshock model, pentylenetetrazol administration, kindling, and bicuculline microinjections in the anterior piriform cortex (area tempestas) (Statnick *et al.*, 1996). Conversely, reduction of brain serotonin concentrations leads to an increase in seizure susceptibility in animal models of epilepsy (Wenger *et al.*, 1973, Lazarova *et al.*, 1983) as well as in humans. In human brain tissue surgically removed for seizure control, the level of 5-HIAA, which is a breakdown product of serotonin, was found to be higher in actively spiking temporal cortex as compared with normal tissue (Pintor *et al.*, 1990). Finally, increased serotonin immunoreactivity has been reported in human epileptic brain tissue resected for the control of epilepsy (Trottier *et al.*, 1996). Serotonergic neurotransmission exerts a considerable influence on hippocampal function. It is influenced powerfully by serotonergic projections from midbrain raphe nuclei (Moore & Halaris, 1975; Lidov *et al.*, 1980), which modulate hippocampal electrical activity, hippocampal-dependent behaviours, and long-term potentiation (LTP), a form of hippocampal plasticity that has been implicated in memory formation (Winson, 1980; Bliss *et al.*, 1983). Studies of the serotonergic modulation of hippocampal function have been complicated by the marked heterogeneity of 5-HT receptor subtypes, with at least 14 distinct subtypes expressed in the central nervous system. Determining the contributions of individual 5-HT receptor subtypes to the serotonergic regulation of hippocampal function is hindered by a paucity of subtype-selective drugs (8-12). Studies indicate 5-HT consistently hyperpolarized theophylline-treated hippocampal CA3 neurons and abolished theophylline-induced epileptiform activity. Efforts to determine the mechanisms through which serotonin (5-HT) systems regulate CNS excitability have been complicated by the marked diversity of 5-HT receptor subtypes and the paucity of available selective agonists and antagonists. At least 14 distinct 5-HT receptor subtypes have been identified in the CNS and there are few selective pharmacological agents available to determine the functional roles of individual receptor subtypes.

Central 5-HT$_{1A}$ receptors function both as somatodendric presynaptic autoreceptors in the raphe nuclei as postsynaptic receptors in terminal field areas such as the hippocampus and many have different functional and regulatory characteristics, depending on the structures innervated (Barnes *et al.*, 1999). In the raphe nuclei activation of 5-HT$_{1A}$ autoreceptors produces inhibition of serotonergic neurons and decreases 5-HT release and neurotransmission. In contrast, postsynaptic 5-HT$_{1A}$ receptor activation in the hippocampus increases 5-HT neurotransmission (Clarke *et al.*, 1996). The 5-HT$_{1A}$ somatodendric autoreceptors and postsynaptic receptors differ in their adaptive response to prolonged stimulation during long term treatment with selective serotonin reuptake inhibitors (SSRIs) such as fluoxetine, which has antiseizure effects in several models (Hernandez *et al.*, 2002). The fluoxetine effect is not dependent on GABA receptors are mediated by multiple receptor subtypes and shows regional variation (Pasini *et al.*, 1996). Rats treated over the long term with fluoxetine showed desensitation of 5-HT$_{1A}$ somatodendric autoreceptors in the dorsal raphe nucleus but not of postsynaptic 5-HT$_{1A}$ receptors in the hippocampus (Le Poul *et al.*, 2000). 5-HT$_{1A}$ receptor activation elicits a membrane hyper polarization response related to increase potassium conductance (Beck *et al.*, 1991) and has an anticonvulsant effect in various experimental *in vivo* as well as *in vitro* seizure models. Including hippocampal kindled seizures in cats, intrahippocampal kainic acid induced seizures in freely moving rats and picrotoxin-bicuculline and kainic acid induced seizures in rat hippocampal slice preparations (Wada *et al.*, 1992). The anticonvulsant effects of 5-HT$_{1A}$ receptor activation differ from region to region and from model to model. 5-HT is reported to inhibit low Mg^{2+}-induced epileptiform activity, by reduction of NMDA receptor-mediated excitatory postsynaptic potentials in the subiculum and entorhinal cortex but not on areas CA3 and CA1 of hippocampus (Behr *et al.*, 1996). The genetically epilepsy prone rat model (GEPR) illustrates 5-HT effects on seizure susceptibility. GEPRs have decreased 5-HT_{1A} receptor density in the hippocampus compared to non epileptic control rats (Statnick *et al.*, 1996). In addition the SSRI sertraline produces a dose dependent reduction in the intensity of audiogenic seizures in GEPRs, correlating with increased extracellular thalamic 5-HT concentrations (Yan *et al.*, 1995). However the model is complex and other neurotransmitters play a role, as 5-HT receptor activation increases release of catecholamines (Yan *et al.*, 1998). 5-HT_{1B} receptor was reported to inhibit rat ventral tegmental GABA release and $5\text{-HT}_{1B/1D}$ activation increases nucleus accumbens dopamine release (Yan *et al.*, 2001). Other receptor subtypes have received less attention. One study suggested an excitatory role of 5-HT3 receptors in a rat kindling model (Wada *et al.*, 1997). Several knock out mouse models suggest a relation between 5-HT, hippocampal dysfunction and epilepsy. 5-HT_{1A} knockout mice display lower seizure thresholds and higher lethality in response to kainic acid administration. Furthermore, 5-HT_{1A} knockout mouse demonstrate impaired hippocampal dependent learning and enhanced anxiety related behaviours. Interactions between serotonergic and other neurotransmitters contribute to the behavioural phenotype (Sarnyai *et al.*, 2000). 5-HT_{2C} receptor knockout mice showed a combination of obesity and sound induced seizures. Other receptor types are not altered in this model suggesting that the clinical effects are receptor subtype specific (Heiser *et al.*, 1998). In contrast activation of 5-HT_{2C} receptors potentiates cocaine induced seizures (O'Dell *et al.*, 2000). The up-regulation of 5-HT_{2C} receptors was reported in the brain stem which induces sympathetic stimulation was reported (Pyroja *et al.*, 2007).

5-HT_{2C} Receptors and Epilepsy

The distribution of 5-HT_{2C} receptors and the action of non-selective drugs have prompted speculations that these receptors participate in the processing and integration of sensory information, regulation of central monoaminergic system and modulation of neuroendocrine regulation, feeding behaviour anxiety and cerebrospinal fluid production. Mice devoid of 5-HT$_{2C}$ receptors showed epileptic phenotype (Tecott *et al.*, 1995) associated with sporadic spontaneous seizures that occasionally result in death. Thus 5-HT$_{2C}$ receptors are involved in the neuronal network excitability which alters the threshold of seizure activity. Mice lacking these receptors exhibit increased focal excitability and facilitated propagation of seizure activity within the forebrain seizure system. These mice also exhibit lower thresholds for the expression of generalized seizures of either the tonic or clonic type. Importantly, the 5-HT receptor antagonist, mesulergine (2 or 4 mg/Kg), administered prior to electroshock testing, recapitulated the mutant phenotype in wild-type mice suggests that the seizure susceptibility profiles observed in 5-HT$_{2C}$ deficient mice are not secondary to developmental abnormalities caused by deletion of the gene (Applegate & Tecott, 1998). Together, these data strongly implicate a role for serotonin and the 5-HT$_{2C}$ receptors in the modulation of neuronal network excitability and seizure propagation throughout the CNS. Reduction in seizure activity has been observed for the 5-HT$_{2C}$ receptor agonists meta-chlorophenylpiperazine (mCPP) and 3-Trifluoromethylphenylpiperazine monohydrochloride (TFMPP) when microinjected bilaterally into the rat substantia nigra. This indicates that the 5-HT$_{2C}$ receptors in the substantia nigra contribute to seizure regulation (Gobert *et al.*, 2000; Hutson *et al.*, 2000). Serotonin 5-HT$_{2C}$ receptors, which play an important role in the control of mood, reward, motor function, and appetite, are implicated in the etiology and management of depression, anxiety, schizophrenia and other psychiatric disorders (Giorgetti & Tecott, 2004; Millan, 2005; Di Giovanni *et al.*, 2006; Dutton & Barnes, 2006). Functional status of 5- HT$_{2C}$ receptors is elevated in depressed patients, in rat models of depression and upon experimental depletion of 5-HT (Heslop & Curzon, 1999; Millan, 2006).

Glutamate

Glutamate is a fast excitatory neurotransmitter in the CNS and has been shown, with GABA, to interact primarily with receptors in the synaptic cleft (Dingledine & McBain, 1999). L-Glutamate is a non-essential dicarboxylic amino acid synthesized mainly from 2-oxoglutarate by transamination reactions. Glutamate has strong excitatory effects on neurons. High affinity uptake systems move them into nerve endings. The occurrence of their receptors is known from sites where radiolabeled glutamate selectively binds on neural cell surfaces and through the discovery of their antagonists. Both procedures identify and characterize their receptors on neuronal and glial cells. These amino acids open sodium and potassium ion channels and cause a rapid excitatory response in most neurons at a very low concentration (Dingledine & McBain, 1999). Electrical stimulation of brain slices and cultured neurons releases glutamate in a Ca^{2+} dependent manner.

Glutamate is the main excitatory amino acid neurotransmitter in central and peripheral nervous systems. Its concentration in brain is higher than in other body tissues. In the brain, the concentration of glutamate is 3 to 4-fold greater than that of aspartate, taurine, or glutamine. The most abundant amino acid in synaptosomes is glutamate, followed by glutamine, aspartate, γ–aminobutyric acid and taurine. Glutamate cannot cross the blood-brain-barrier. The main source of glutamate carbon is glucose with synthesis of glutamate from glucose and other metabolites of the citric acid cycle. It appears however, that aspartate aminotransferase and glutaminase account for a majority of glutamate production in brain tissue (McGeer *et al.*, 1987). Enzymes responsible for the synthesis of glutamate are in neurons as well as glial cells. A large proportion of the glutamate present in the brain is produced by astrocytes through synthesis *de novo* (Hertz *et al.*, 1999), but levels of glutamate in glial cells are lower than in neurons, 2–3 mM and 5–6 mM, respectively. During excitatory neurotransmission, glutamate-filled vesicles are docked at a specialized region of the presynaptic plasma membrane known as the active zone. Packaging and storage of glutamate into glutamatergic neuronal vesicles requires Mg^{2+}/ATP-dependent vesicular glutamate uptake systems, which utilize an electrochemical proton gradient as a driving force. Substances that disturb the electrochemical gradient inhibit this glutamate uptake into vesicles. The concentration of glutamate in vesicle reaches as high as 20–100 mM (Nicholls & Attwell, 1990). In brain tissue, low concentrations of glutamate and aspartate perform as neurotransmitters, but at high concentration these amino acids act as neurotoxins. Many experiments have supported the view that the extent of glutamate release during epileptic seizures is so great that uptake is not able to re-establish the normal glutamate concentration and the excess of glutamate spreads by diffusion, activating neurons *via* extra-synaptic receptors. Increased glutamatergic transmission is regarded as one of the possible causes of seizure origination (Bradford, 1995). Most of the damage induced by seizure activity is generated by glutamatergic neurotransmission-driven excitotoxicity (Whetsell, 1996).

It activates two main types of postsynaptic receptors: (i) ionotropic glutamate receptors (iGluRs) that are ligand-gated channels, and (ii) metabotropic glutamate receptors (mGluRs) that are receptors coupled to GTP binding proteins. The extracellular accumulation of glutamate results in neuronal death by activating ionotropic glutamate receptors sensitive to NMDA or AMPA–KA (Choi, 1988). Ionotropic glutamate receptors are divided into three major subtypes, on the basis of their affinity for glutamate selective structural analogues, notably for N-methyl- D-aspartate (NMDA). A distinction is made between those glutamate receptors activated by NMDA receptors and those not activated by NMDA, non-NMDA receptors. Cloning studies have demonstrated that these non-NMDA receptors can be further distinguished in AMPA and kainate receptors.

Glutamate and Glutamate Receptors in Epilepsy

Glutamate can cause convulsions when administered focally or systemically to experimental animals. Glutamate exerts its excitatory action *via* ligand-gated ion channels, NMDA and non-NMDA receptors, to increase sodium and calcium conductance. Reciprocal regulatory interactions exist between the activation of glutamatergic receptors and other transmitter systems, ion transport, gene activation and receptor modification. The flexibility and complexity of these interactions place glutamate-mediated transmission in a pivotal position for modulating the excitatory threshold of pathways involved in seizure generation. All classes of NMDA receptor antagonists, competitive NMDA antagonists, channel site antagonists, glycine site antagonists, polyamine site antagonists, as well as competitive and noncompetitive AMPA/kainate antagonists, display wide-spectrum anticonvulsant properties in acute and chronic animal epilepsy models, with varying degrees of behavioural side effects, ranging from minimal for some of the glycine site or competitive NMDA antagonists, to extensive for some of the high affinity open-channel NMDA antagonists. Transgenic mice with an editing-deficient AMPA receptor subunit, $GluR_2$, display early onset of epilepsy. The $GluR_2$ subunit confers an almost complete block of calcium conductance in homomeric or heteromeric AMPA receptors. Both the $GluR_2$ receptor level and the RNA editing process are reduced significantly and the corresponding AMPA-evoked calcium current in pyramidal neurons increased significantly in accordance with the enhanced seizure susceptibility in these mice (Brusa *et al.*, 1995). Neuronal (EAAC-1) and glial (GLT-1 and GLAST) glutamate transporters facilitate glutamate and aspartate reuptake after synaptic release. A down regulation of glutamate transporters would be compatible with enhanced excitatory activity. Transgenic mice with GLT-1 knockout display spontaneous epileptic activity (Tanaka *et al.*, 1997) and mice treated chronically with antisense probes to EAAC-1 shows reduced transporter levels and increased epileptic activity (Rothstein *et al.*, 1996). The reported changes in glutamate receptors and transporters subsequent to sustained or chronic epilepsy are less consistent and frequently transient in nature; some of these changes reflect patterns of cell loss. A functional enhancement of NMDA receptors is observed in amygdala-kindled rats and in resected tissue from humans with temporal lobe epilepsy (Mody *et al.*, 1998). The molecular alterations in the NMDA receptor responsible for this functional up regulation are not clearly defined but probably involve altered phosphorylation. Changes in the editing of the GluR2 AMPA subunit been reported in resected hippocampi from some patients with refractory epilepsy (Grigorenko *et al.*, 1997). The mRNA levels of multiple AMPA subunits are also altered in kindled rats and in rats after sustained seizure activity evoked by kainate or pilocarpine.

Ionotropic Receptors - NMDA Receptors

The discovery of potent and selective agonists and antagonists has resulted in extensive information on the NMDA receptor-channel complex (Wood *et al.*, 1990). It consists of four domains:- (1) the transmitter recognition site with which NMDA and L-glutamate interact; (2) a cation binding site located inside the channel where Mg^{2+} can bind and block transmembrane ion fluxes; (3) a PCP binding site that requires agonist binding to the transmitter recognition site, interacts with the cation binding site, and at which a number of dissociative anesthetics PCP and ketamine, □opiate N-allylnormetazocine (SKF-10047) and MK-801 bind and function as open channel blockers; and (4) a glycine binding site that appears to allosterically modulate the interaction between the transmitter recognition site and the PCP binding site (Fagg & Baud, 1988). NMDA is allosterically modulated by glycine, a co-agonist whose presence is an absolute requirement for receptor activation. Molecular cloning has identified to date cDNAs encoding NR_1 and NR2A, B, C, D subunits of the NMDA receptor, the deduced amino acid sequences of which are 18% belonging to NR1 and NR2, 55% belonging to NR2A and NR_2C or 70% belonging to NR2A and NR2B are identical. Site-directed mutagenesis has revealed that the NR2 subunit carries the binding site for glutamate within the N-terminal domain and the extracellular loop between membrane segments M3 and M4; whereas the homologous domains of the NR1 subunit carry the binding site for the co-agonist glycine.

Normal functioning of the NMDA receptor complex depends on a dynamic equilibrium among various domain components. Loss of equilibrium during membrane perturbation cause the entire system to malfunction and result in abnormal levels of glutamate in the synaptic cleft (Olney, 1989). An important consequence of NMDA receptor activation is the influx of Ca^{2+} into neurons (Murphy & Miller, 1988; Holopainen *et al.*, 1989, 1990; MacDermott *et al.*, 1986). Collective evidence suggests that when the membrane is depolarized, the Mg^{2+} block is relieved and the receptor can be activated by glutamate. Activation of the NMDA receptor therefore requires the association of two synaptic events: membrane depolarization and glutamate release. This associative property provides the logic for the role of the NMDA receptor in sensory integration, memory function, coordination and programming of motor activity (Collingridge & Bliss, 1987; Lester *et al.*, 1988) associated with synaptogenesis and synaptic plasticity.

Functional Effects Mediated *Via* the NMDA Receptor Signal Transduction

The NMDA class of glutamate receptors has a critical role in the induction of long-term potentiation (LTP), a synaptic modification that encode some forms of long-term memory. However, NMDA receptor antagonists disrupt a variety of mental processes (Caramanos & Shapiro, 1994; Verma & Moghaddam, 1996; Javitt *et al.*, 1996) that are not dependent on long-term memory. They interfere with working memory (Krystal *et al.*, 1994; Adler *et al.*, 1998) a short-lasting form of memory that is maintained by neuronal activity rather than by synaptic modification. This suggests that there are unknown functions of the NMDA-receptor channel. Working memory is stored by the maintained firing of a memory- specific subset of neurons in networks of the prefrontal cortex (Funahashi *et al.*, 1989). Firing is thought to be maintained by a reverberatory process (Amit *et al.*, 1994) in which active neurons selectively excites each other through recurrent connections. The NMDA receptor in the forebrain is thought to modulate some forms of memory formation, with the NR_{2B} subunit being particularly relevant to this process.

NMDA receptors and Epilepsy

Several studies have shown an increase in the density of hippocampal and cortical NMDA receptors in some animal models of epilepsy (Yeh *et al.*, 1989; Corlew *et al.*, 2008). This up regulation reflects one molecular mechanism that maintains neuronal hyperexcitability in the course of the epileptic disease and is implicated in NMDAR-targeted therapies treating seizure disorders (Kalia *et al.*, 2008). Epileptogenesis causes an $NMDA/Ca^{2+}$- dependent decrease in $Ca^{2+/}$calmodulin-dependent protein kinase II activity in a hippocampal neuronal culture model of spontaneous recurrent epileptiform discharges. When epileptiform activity is acutely induced in vitro, transient partial blockade of NMDA receptor-mediated calcium influx leads to selective long-term depotentiation of the synapses involved in the epileptic activity as well as a reduction in the probability of further epileptiform activity (Hellier *et al.*, 2009). In postsynaptic densities isolated from epileptic human and rat neocortex, however, components of the NMDA-receptor complex were found to be down regulated (Wyneken *et al.*, 2003).

Metabotropic Glutamate Receptors

Metabotropic glutamate (mGlu) receptors have a widespread distribution throughout the CNS and are understood to be involved in a number of physiological mechanisms including memory, learning and motor control. The mGluRs comprise a novel family of G-protein coupled receptors, which are characterized by a large ligand-binding N-terminal domain and seven transmembrane domains responsible for

G-protein coupling. The second intracellular loop of mGluRs determines G-protein coupling specificity, while other intracellular loops contribute to coupling efficiency. This differs somewhat from other G-protein coupled receptor families. Metabotropic glutamate receptors are classified into three groups based on their amino acid sequence homology, signal transduction mechanisms and pharmacology (Pin & Duvoisin, 1995).

Group I mGlu receptors (mGlu1/5) are positively coupled to phospholipase C (PLC) and induce the hydrolysis of phosphoinositide and the release of intracellular Ca^{2+} stores. Group II mGlu receptors (mGlu2/3) are negatively coupled to adenylate cyclase (AC) and have been shown to inhibit the production of cAMP and Ca^{2+} influx. Group III mGlu receptors (mGlu4, 6–8) are thought to be similarly coupled to AC and inhibit the production of cAMP. At least eight metabotropic glutamate receptors (mGluR1-8) occur in brain tissue. They are members of the group C family of G-protein-coupled receptors, GPCR (Bonsi *et al.*, 2005). Based on sequence homology, agonist pharmacology and coupling to intracellular transduction mechanisms, metabotropic receptors are classified into three groups (Endoh, 2004). In the recent past, evidence accumulated in favour of a central role of group I mGlu receptors (Bonsia, 2008).

Group I consists of mGluR1 and mGluR5, including their splice variants. These receptors are coupled to an inositol phosphate/Ca^{2+} intracellular signaling pathway. These receptors are found on postsynaptic membranes (Endoh, 2004). In general, group-I mGluRs tend to increase neuronal excitability by inhibiting potassium conductances and activating non-selective cation currents. Conversely, mGluRs in groups II and III reduce neuronal excitability by activating potassium currents. They are involved in the modulation of the permeability of Na^+ channels and K^+ channels. Their action can be excitatory, increasing conductance, causing more glutamate to be released from the presynaptic cell, but they also increase inhibitory postsynaptic potentials (Chu & Hablitz, 2000). They can also inhibit glutamate release and can modulate voltage dependent Ca^{2+} channels (Endoh, 2004).

Metabotropic glutamate mGlu5 receptors have been implicated in the regulation of seizures and have been suggested as a target against which discovery of novel anticonvulsants may be possible. However, the experimental literature is not consistent in reporting anticonvulsant efficacy of mGlu5 receptor antagonists. But studies by Witkin *et al.*, (2008) do not support the idea that mGlu5 receptors play as important a role in seizure control as previously speculated.

Glutamate Transporter

Glutamate transport is the major mechanism controlling extracellular glutamate levels, preventing excitotoxicity and averting neural damage associated with epilepsy. (McBean & Roberts, 1985; Rothstein *et al.*, 1992, 1994, 1995; Robinson *et al.*, 1993; Tanaka *et al.*, 1997). Glutamate transporters are localized to the membranes of synaptic terminals and astroglial processes that ensheath synaptic complexes (Kanner & Schuldiner, 1987; Danbolt *et al.*, 1992; Kanai *et al.*, 1993; Rothstein *et al.*, 1994, 1996; Conti *et al.*, 1998). GLAST for glutamate–aspartate transporter, (EAAT-1) for excitatory amino acid transporter-1 (Storck *et al.*, 1992; Arriza *et al.*, 1994) and GLT-1 for glutamate transporter-1, EAAT-2 (Pines *et al.*, 1992; Arriza *et al.*, 1994) are astroglial glutamate transporters, and EAAC1 for excitatory amino acid carrier-1, EAAT-3 (Kanai & Hediger, 1992; Arriza *et al.*, 1994; Shashidharan *et al.*, 1994; Kanai *et al.*, 1995; Bjoras *et al.*, 1996; Nakayama *et al.*, 1996; Velaz-Faircloth *et al.*, 1996; Eskandari *et al.*, 2000), EAAT-4 (Fairman *et al.*, 1995) and EAAT-5 (Arriza *et al.*, 1997) are neuronal proteins.

Signal transduction through Second Messengers

Inositol 1,4,5-trisphosphate (IP3)

Many biological stimuli, such as neurotransmitters, hormones and growth factors, activate the hydrolysis of phosphatidyl inositol 4,5-bisphosphate (PIP2) in the plasma membrane which is hydrolyzed by phospholipase C (PLC) to produce IP3 and diacylglycerol (DAG). The IP3 mediates Ca^{2+} release from intracellular Ca^{2+} stores by binding to IP3 receptors (IP3R). IP3R are the IP3 gated intracellular Ca^{2+} channels that are mainly present in the endoplasmic reticulum (ER) membrane. The IP3 induced Ca^{2+} signaling plays a crucial role in the control of diverse physiological processes such as contraction, secretion, gene expression and synaptic plasticity (Berridge, 1993). In response to many stimuli such as neurotransmitters, hormones and growth factors, PIP2 in the plasma membrane is hydrolyzed by PLC to produce IP3 and diacylglycerol (DAG). IP3 plays a dominant role as a second messenger molecule for the release of Ca^{2+} from intracellular stores, while DAG activates protein kinase C (PKC).

In mammalian cells, there are three IP3R subtypes- IP3R1, IP3R2 and IP3R3 which are expressed to varying degrees in individual cell types (Wojcikiewicz, 1995; Taylor *et al.*, 1999) and form homotetrameric or heterotetrameric channels (Monkawa *et al.*, 1995). In previous studies, a plasmid vector containing full-length rat IP3R3 linked to green fluorescent protein GFP-IP3R3 was constructed and visualized the distribution of GFP-IP3R3 was constructed in living cells (Morita *et al.*, 2002, 2004). The confocal images obtained in these studies provided strong evidence that IP3Rs are distributed preferentially on the ER network. Furthermore, Morita *et al.*, (2004) demonstrated that the expressed GFP-IP3R3 acts as a functional IP3-induced Ca^{2+} channel. Frequently, IP3Rs are not uniformly distributed over the membrane but rather form discrete clusters (Bootman *et al.*, 1997). The clustered distribution of IP3Rs has been predicted to be important in controlling elementary Ca^{2+} release events, such as Ca^{2+} puffs and blips, which act as triggers to induce the spatiotemporal patterns of global Ca^{2+} signals, such as waves and oscillations (Thomas *et al.*, 1998; Swillens *et al.*, 1999; Shuai & Jung, 2003). Tateishi *et al.*, (2005) reported that GFP-IP3R1 expressed in COS-7 cells aggregates into clusters on the ER network after agonist stimulation. They concluded that IP3R clustering is induced by its IP3-induced conformational change to the open state, not by Ca^{2+} release itself, because IP3R1 mutants that do not undergo an IP3 induced conformational change failed to form clusters. However, their results are inconsistent with studies by other groups (Wilson *et al.*, 1998; Chalmers *et al.*, 2006), which suggested that IP3R clustering is dependent on the continuous elevation of intracellular Ca^{2+} concentration. Thus, the precise mechanism underlying IP3R clustering remains controversial. Studies by Tojyo *et al.*, (2008) have shown that IP3 binding to IP3R, not the increase in $[Ca^{2+}]i$, is absolutely critical for IP3R clustering. They also found that depletion of intracellular Ca^{2+} stores facilitates the generation of agonist-induced IP3R clustering.

Group I mGluRs (mGluR1/5 subtypes) are also demonstrated to mainly affect intracellular Ca^{2+} mobilization (Conn & Pin, 1997; Bordi & Ugolini, 1999). To sequentially facilitate intracellular Ca^{2+} release, group I receptors activate the membrane-bound phospholipase C (PLC), which stimulates phosphoinositide turnover by hydrolyzing PIP2 to IP3 and diacylglycerol. IP3 then causes the release of Ca^{2+} from intracellular Ca^{2+} stores (such as endoplasmic reticulum) by binding to specific IP3 receptors on the membrane of Ca^{2+} stores (Berridge, 1993). Altered Ca^{2+} levels could then engage in the modulation of broad cellular activities.

Cyclic Guanosine Monophosphate (cGMP)

cGMP generation has been associated with neurotransmission (Hofmann *et al.*, 2000), vascular smooth muscle relaxation (Fiscus *et al.*, 1985) and inhibition of aldosterone release from adrenal glomerulosa cell suspension (Matsuoka *et al.*, 1985). The most extensively studied cGMP signal transduction pathway is that triggered by nitric oxide (NO) (Bredt & Snyder, 1990). cGMP effects are primarily mediated by the activation of cGMP-dependent protein kinases (PKGs). Two distinct mammalian PKGs- PKG-I and PKG-II- have been identified, as well as two splice variants of PKG-I - PKG-Iα and -Iβ. In the brain, PKG-I is highly expressed in cerebellar Purkinje cells and to a lesser extent, in striatal medium spiny neurons (De Camilli *et al.*, 1984). PKG-II is a membrane-associated protein that is expressed throughout the brain (de Vente *et al.*, 2001). The effects produced by the cGMP signaling pathway modulate drug-induced neural plasticity leading to behavioural alterations (Jouvert *et al.*, 2004).

Activation of the NMDA receptor increases cAMP in the CA1 region of the hippocampus; this increase is mediated through Ca^{2+} calmodulin-dependent adenylyl cyclase (Chetkovich & Sweatt, 1993). The influx of Ca^{2+} also stimulates Ca^{2+} calmodulin-dependent nitric-oxide synthase (NOS) type to produce NO, which stimulates guanylyl cyclase to produce cGMP (Garthwaite, 1991).

Cyclic nucleotide pathways can cross talk to modulate each other's synthesis, degradation and actions. Increased cGMP can increase the activity of cGMP stimulated PDE2 to enhance hydrolysis of cAMP, or it can inhibit the PDE3 family and decrease the hydrolysis of cAMP (Pelligrino & Wang, 1998). cAMP and cGMP are involved in NMDA receptor-mediated signaling in cerebral cortical and hippocampal neuronal cultures. The influx of Ca^{2+} *via* the NMDA receptor stimulates calcium/calmodulin dependent adenylyl cyclase, leading to production of cAMP. This increase in cAMP seems to be tightly regulated by PDE4. The Ca^{2+} influx also stimulates the production of NO and subsequent activation of guanylyl cyclase, leading to cGMP production (Suvarna & O'Donnell, 2002).

Cyclic Adenosine Monophosphate (cAMP)

The second messenger concept of signaling was born with the discovery of cAMP and its ability to influence metabolism, cell shape and gene transcription (Sutherland, 1972) *via* reversible protein phosphorylations. cAMP is produced from

ATP adenylyl cyclase (AC) in response to a variety of extracellular signals such as hormones, growth factors and neurotransmitters. Elevated levels of cAMP in the cell lead to activation of different cAMP targets. It was long thought that the only target of cAMP was the cAMP-dependent protein kinase (cAPK), which has become a model of protein kinase structure and regulation (Francis & Corbin, 1999; Canaves & Taylor, 2002). In recent years it has become clear that not all effects of cAMP are mediated by a general activation of cAPK (Dremier *et al.*, 1997). Several cAMP binding proteins have been described: cAPK (Walsh *et al.*, 1968), the cAMP receptor of *Dictyostelium discoideum*, which participates in the regulation of development (Klein *et al.*, 1998), cyclic nucleotide gated channels involved in transduction of olfactory and visual signals (Goulding *et al.*, 1992; Kaupp *et al.*, 1989) and the cAMP-activated guanine exchange factors Epac 1,2 which specifically activate the monomeric G protein Rap (Rooij *et al.*, 1998; Kawasaki,*et al.*, 1998).

Pathophysiology of Temporal Lobe Epilepsy

EEG studies shows that the hippocampus is one of the earliest structures to be activated during seizures. In addition, the cure of epilepsy by surgical resection of the hippocampus in properly selected individuals led to the idea that hyperexcitability intrinsic to the hippocampus contribute to the development of epilepsy (Bausch & McNamara, 1999). Thus it is not surprising that from the perspective of mechanisms, the best studied form of seizure is the seizure activity in the hippocampus. Recent report states that different neuronal populations react differently to SE induction. For some brain areas most, if not all, of the vulnerable cells are lost after an initial insult leaving only relatively resistant cells and little space for further damage or cell loss (Covolan *et al.*, 2006).

Cell Loss

The most frequent lesion in patients with TLE is mesial temporal sclerosis or hippocampal sclerosis, consisting of gliosis and neuronal loss in the CA1, CA3 and the hilus of the dentate gyrus (Houser *et al.*, 1990). This typical pattern of neuronal loss characteristic of hippocampal sclerosis (Kapur *et al*, 1999; Lewis *et al.*, 1999) can be produced experimentally by repeated or prolonged seizures and results presumably from excitotoxic damage subsequent to excessive activation of glutamate receptors (Olney *et al.*, 1986; Sloviter *et al.*, 1994). There are striking similarities between the pathology produced in experimental animals by prolonged seizures (Sloviter *et al.*, 1991) or head trauma (Coulter *et al.*, 1996) and the pathological changes seen in the hippocampi of many patients with TLE (Meldrum & Bruton, 1992). Seven days and two months post-status epilepticus rats showed significant neuron loss in the pre-endopiriform nucleus, layer III of the intermediate piriform cortex, and layers II and III of the caudal piriform cortex (Chen *et al.*, 2007). There is an extensive loss of dentate hilar neurons (Bausch & Chavkin., 1997) and hippocampal pyramidal cells (De Giorgio *et al.*, 1997). Data also demonstrated cases where some granule cells of experimental animals are also highly vulnerable (Sloviter *et al.*, 1996). Seizure-induced astrocytic damage has also been documented (Schmidt-Kastner & Ingvar, 1996). Interestingly, in contrast to the many studies showing cell loss, a recent study described an increased generation of hippocampal granule cells as a consequence of seizures (Parent *et al.*, 1997). It is hypothesized that the astrocytes in sclerotic tissue have activated molecular pathways that could lead to enhanced release of glutamate by these cells. Such glutamate release may excite surrounding neurons and elicit seizure activity (Janigro, 2008). Induction of limbic epilepsy resulted in an increased proliferation of granule cells using bromodeoxyuridine labelling. Therefore, although death of certain cell populations was suggested as a main event during or as a result of epileptogenesis, there is also evidence of neurogenesis. Mechanistically, neuronal loss can occur with either active or passive participation of cellular constituents. This has been referred to as apoptosis or necrosis (Kerr *et al.*, 1972). Apoptosis is a form of gene-mediated death characterised by specific morphological features: early nuclear chromatin condensation, Cytoplasmic compaction with cell shrinkage, endonuclease-mediated DNA fragmentation into oligonucleosomes, apoptotic body formation and well-preserved organelles. In contrast, necrosis resulting from sudden injury with the cell unable to maintain homeostasis is characterized by early cytoplasmic vacuolization before any nuclear changes occurs and is associated with an inflammatory response (Tomei & Cope, 1991). It appears that epileptic neuronal death is primarily but not exclusively apoptotic (Charriaut-Marlangue & Ben-Ari, 1995). Long-term repetitive stimulation of the perforant path induced apoptosis in the granule cells but necrosis in the hilar and pyramidal cells (Sloviter *et al.*, 1996). The surviving granule cells showed dendritic deformations and shrinkage (Isokawa & Mello, 1991).

Axon sprouting

In addition to the neuronal loss, the second morphological change induced in the hippocampus by seizures is sprouting of dentate granule cell axons which are commonly referred to as mossy fibres. This occurs in both animal models of epilepsy (Bausch & Chavkin, 1997) as well as in human epilepsy (Babb *et al.*, 1991). Denervation of the inner molecular layer secondary to hilar cell loss is believed to constitute the initial stimulus for sprouting (Tauck & Nadler, 1985). The sprouted mossy fibre axons appear to make synaptic contacts with granule cells and GABAergic basket cells. It has been proposed that seizure induced expression of neurotropic genes which is suggested to underlie the sprouting of axons of the granule cell layer (Sutula *et al.*, 1996). It has been established that nerve growth factor (NGF) protein levels in dentate granule cells are increased by seizure activity (Gall & Isackson, 1989).

Gliosis

Reactive gliosis occurs in response to injury, including pilocarpine- induced seizures, in the mature CNS. A salient manifestation of reactive gliosis is an increase in glial fibrillary acidic protein (GFAP), a protein subunit of glial intermediate filaments found exclusively in astrocytes in the CNS (Amaducci *et al.*, 1981). Glial proliferation characteristically accompanies neuronal loss seen in Ammon's horn sclerosis and after various insults including status epilepticus and contributes to epileptogenesis.

Dendritic Changes

Dendritic degeneration is another common pathological finding in TLE and its animal models (Isokawa *et al.*, 1998). Neurons from the hippocampus and neocortex from patients with chronic focal epilepsy showed dramatic dendritic abnormalities. Dendritic spine loss has been repeatedly reported and has been suggested to be more severe with an increased duration of a seizure disorder (Multani *et al.*, 1994). Dendrites of pyramidal cells have also been reported to have varicose swellings at irregular intervals along their length (Muller *et al.*, 1993). It was established that following initial acute seizures, surviving neurons undergo substantial changes in the morphology and density of dendrites and spines in the chronic phase, during which the gradual development of spontaneous seizure is established (Isokawa *et al.*, 1998). In the pilocarpine animal model of epilepsy, the membrane time constant of neurons, which can assess a cells total surface area and geographic extent of dendritic branches was reported to be significantly reduced in rats that experienced many spontaneous seizures in the chronic phase (Isokawa *et al.*, 1996). This suggests that the higher the frequency of spontaneous seizures, the more severe the local dendritic shrinkage.

Mossy fibre sprouting and impaired inhibition.

Mossy fiber sprouting is a form of synaptic reorganization in the dentate gyrus that occurs in human temporal lobe epilepsy and animal models of epilepsy. The axons of dentate gyrus granule cells, called mossy fibers, develop collaterals that grow into an abnormal location, the inner third of the dentate gyrus molecular layer. Electron microscopy has shown that sprouted fibers form synapses on both spines and dendritic shafts in the inner molecular layer, which are likely to represent the dendrites of granule cells and inhibitory neurons. One of the controversies about this phenomenon is whether mossy fiber sprouting contributes to seizures by forming novel recurrent excitatory circuits among granule cells. Sprouting mossy fibers synapse almost exclusively with excitatory neurons in the granule cell layer and molecular layer of the dentate gyrus. Lesioning the synaptic input from the entorhinal cortex to granule cells also triggers mossy fiber sprouting and synaptogenesis in adult rats (Laurberg & Zimmer, 1981; Frotscher & Zimmer, 1983). A variety of experimental treatments that produce epilepsy also induce axon sprouting in other brain regions (Salin *et al.*, 1995; Perez *et al.*, 1996; McKinney *et al.*, 1997; Esclapez *et al.*, 1999). Repeated intense seizures caused an attenuation of GABA mediated inhibition of the granule cells and in the pyramidal cells of the hippocampus (Coulter *et al.*, 1996). This change cannot be explained by a selective loss of GABAergic inhibitory interneuron, since the GABA immunoreactive neurons were shown to be more resistant to seizure-induced injury than other hippocampal neurons (Sloviter *et al.*, 1987). Preservation of GABAergic cells in surgical specimens from patients with epilepsy was confirmed (Babb *et al.*, 1989). The neurons among the most sensitive to the seizure-induced neuronal death are the mossy cells in the dentate hilus (Lowenstrin *et al.*, 1992; Sloviter *et al.*, 1989). These cells receive synaptic input from granule cells *via* collaterals of mossy fibres and from the entorhinal cortex *via* the perforant path. To account for the paradoxical loss of GABA-mediated inhibition with preservation of GABAergic neurons, the dormant basket cell hypothesis (Sloviter *et al.*, 1987) suggests that the seizure-induced loss of hilar excitatory neurons removes tonic excitatory projection to GABAergic basket cells, the inhibitory interneuron in the dentate hilus. Being deafferented these cells then lie dormant with the end result being disinhibition (Sloviter *et al.*, 1987). Loss of mossy cells which govern lateral inhibition in the dentate area cause functional delamination of the granule cell layer and result in synchronous multilamellar discharges in response to excitatory input (Sloviter *et al.*, 1994). Therefore, there are 3 premises to this theory: 1) the general preservation of the inhibitory network. 2) The loss of excitatory afferents to GABAergic interneuron, 3) decreased inhibition on principal cells (Bernard *et al.*, 1998).

Epilepsy and personality disorder

An epileptic phenomenon that illustrates this point is the partial epileptic seizure, which can secondarily generalize. The partial epileptic seizure is a neuronal network phenomenon rather than just a simple focus of hyperactive cells, as once thought. When partial seizure begins, the activated network from which the aberrant properties emerge is relatively localized, resulting in a relatively minor, usually non-convulsive pattern of behaviours (e.g. automatisms). However, if the seizure secondarily generalizes, the neuronal network of the seizure undergoes expansion and additional networks (e.g. locomotion networks) become recruited. Dependency is one of the most common psychological characteristics of patients with epilepsy. It is a disabling disorder that induces a sense of decreased control and self-efficacy, social difficulties, a perception of being stigmatized and low self-esteem (Teddman *et al.*, 1994; Collins, 1994). Individuals with epilepsy have higher incidence of psychiatric disorders than do those without epilepsy. Depression is the most frequently reported psychiatric condition in epileptic patients.

Depression represents one of the most common co-morbidities in patients with epilepsy. However, the mechanisms of depression in epilepsy patients are poorly understood. Establishment of animal models of this co-morbidity is critical for both understanding the mechanisms of the condition, and for preclinical development of effective therapies.

Neuroprotection and Drugs in Epilepsy

Neuroprotection following status epilepticus should encompass not only the prevention of neuronal death, but also preservation of neuronal and network function. This is critical because these aims are not necessarily equivalent; prevention of neuronal loss, for example, does not inevitably prevent epileptogenesis. Anticonvulsant drugs prevent or terminate seizures. In so doing, these agents act on the emergent properties of the epileptogenic network to alter or diminish their function (Walker, 2007). This involves modification of specific neuronal components that result in sufficient elevation of seizure threshold that prevents the usual initiating mechanisms from activating the network. Such an action can totally prevent the seizure or result in blockade of specific behavioural components of the seizure thereby reducing seizure severity (Graumlich *et al.*, 1999; Faingold, 1999). Long-lasting changes in neuronal networks are observed following repetitive experiences, including behavioural conditioning and repeated seizures. Experience repetition can induce neurogenesis in susceptible brain sites, resulting in structural and functional network changes. Structural changes are partially mediated by neurotrophic factors and excitation increases and burst firing in network neurons can result.

By classifying epilepsy syndromes - seizure type, age of onset, EEG evidence, associated impairments, - clinicians can begin to rationalise their approach and define the therapeutic options for each patient. When to start and/or stop drug treatment in epilepsy is a major issue, which requires detailed knowledge of the prognosis of the disorder. For 20-30% of sufferers, epilepsy is a chronic and disabling condition, refractory to drug treatment, which has immense social impact. Although currently available drugs are able to prevent seizures, there remains a clear unmet medical need for new antiepileptic drugs. **David Chadwick's,**Walton Centre for Neurology, Liverpool defines criteria for the ideal antiepileptic drug (AED):-

- A clearly identified and novel mechanism of action;
- Simple pharmacokinetic profile - no interactions with existing drugs;
- Efficacy across the broad spectrum of seizure types;
- Low toxicity and wide therapeutic window;
- Low cost.

To put things in perspective, 30% of epilepsies are currently uncontrolled. There is little rational basis for use of AEDs and side effects and drug interactions are major problems. Current developments in mechanism based drug design hopefully will overcome these issues and allow for more confidence in therapy. Experiments in intact animals provide a complementary approach for the application of mechanistic information obtained in *in vitro* investigations. *In vivo* techniques allow the exploration of the regional selectivity of these mechanisms, since it has become quite clear that the anticonvulsant effects of certain drugs involve actions on a combination of specific currents and cellular properties selectively expressed in specific brain networks (Kao & Coulter, 1997). Whether such actions observed with acute anticonvulsant drug treatment continue during the duration of treatment is unknown, since it is becoming clear that chronic treatment with a number of drugs that modify neuronal properties often results in compensatory mechanisms that lead to tolerance or to additional chronic effects that contribute to the action of the drug (Chen *et al.*, 1999).

***Bacopa monnieri* (Linn.) Pennel**

Kingdom: Plantae

Division: Magnoliophyta

Class: Magnoliopsida

Order: Lamiales

Family: Scrophulariaceae

Genus: *Bacopa*

Species: *Bacopa monnieri*

The drugs of plant origin are gaining importance and are being investigated for remedies of a number of disorders. Since the introduction of adaptogen concept (Lazarev, 1947), several plants have been investigated, which were used earlier as tonics due to their adaptogenic and rejuvenating properties in traditional medicine (Rege *et al.*, 1999). Effective treatments such as anxiolytic drug therapy or cognitive-behavioural therapy exist but many patients remain untreated, experience adverse effects of benzodiazepines or do not benefit from full symptom control (Ernst, 2006). Commonly known as 'Brahmi', the plant has been used by Ayurvedic medical practitioners in India for almost 3000 years and is classified as a medhyarasayana, a drug used to improve memory and intellect (medhya). *Bacopa monnieri* is highly esteemed as a Rasayana drug in Ayurvedic medicine.

Bacopa monnieri (Linn) (family: Scrophulariaceae) is a perennial creeping annual plant found throughout the Indian subcontinent in wet, damp and marshy areas (Sheikh *et al.*, 2007). The main stem is green or slightly purplish, obtuse-angular and 10-30 cm long with rooting at nodes. Leaves are opposite, short-petioled, obovate-oblong and somewhat succulent 1-2.5 cm long and 0.4-1 cm broad, glabrous on both sides and dotted with minute black specks. Flowers are solitary axially, white or purple-tinged. Fruits are ovoid capsules, about 5 mm long and glabrous. The plant flowers and bears fruits throughout the year, though mostly during February to April. Both fresh and dried whole plant is used for drug preparation.

The plant elaborates several tri-terpenoids of dammarane group which occur mostly as glycosides (saponins) and are present to the extent of 2-3% on dry herb basis and are considered medicinally valuable. Around 10 of these have been obtained pure (Bacosaponins A-F, Bacoposides III-IV). Betulinic acid a tri-terpene with known anticancer activity has also been obtained from the plant (Brown *et al.*, 1960). Four glycosides based on phenylethanol as basic unit have been isolated (Chakravarthy *et al.*, 2002). Of other secondary metabolites attention is drawn to flavonoids like luteolin and its glycosisdes, sugars (D-mannnitol), usual sterols - β-sitosterol, stigmasterol and its esters and paraffins – heptacosane and hentriacontane.

The pharmacological properties of *Bacopa monnieri* were studied extensively and the activities were attributed mainly due to the presence of characteristic saponins called as Bacosides (Deepak & Amit, 2004). Bacosides are complex mixture of structurally closely related compounds, glycosides of either jujubogenin or pseudojujubogenin. Bacosides have been found to offer protective role in the synaptic functions of the nerves in hippocampus (Kishore *et al.*, 2005). There are few methods reported in the literature for quantification of Bacosides in plant extracts and formulations. Spectrophotometric methods (Pal & Sarin, 1992; Prakash *et al.*, 2008) developed based on the hydrolysis of Bacosides to an aglycone that has an absorption maximum at 278 nm. A high performance thin-layer chromatographic method was developed for the estimation of Bacoside A in *Bacopa monnieri* plant and its formulations (Shrikumar *et al.*, 2004). A few high performance liquid chromatographic (HPLC) methods were also developed for the quantification of Bacosides in *Bacopa monnieri* extracts and formulations (Pal *et al.*, 1998).

The whole plant is a potent nerve tonic and is well known for its neuropharmacological effects. It is used in the treatment of epilepsy, insanity, hysteria and other neural disorders. It is claimed to improve memory and mental function. Its neuropharmacological activity (Singh & Dhawan, 1997) and anti-oxidant activities (Singh *et al.*, 2006) has been also reported. After clinical trials in human volunteers, a chemically standardized extract of *Bacopa monnieri* has been now made available for clinical use by the Central Drug Research Institute in India (Dhawan & Singh, 1996). *Bacopa monnieri* has been reported to possess anxiolytic, antidepressant and memory enhancing activity (Bhattacharya & Ghosal, 1998; Bhattacharya *et al.*, 1999; Sairam *et al.*, 2002; Das *et al.*, 2002). Studies by Rai *et al.*, (2003) identified the potential of *Bacopa monnieri* as an effective adaptogen that normalizes the stress induced elevation in plasma glucose, creatine kinase and adrenal gland weight similar to the effects of *Panax quinquefolium* (PQ), commonly known as American ginseng, a standard adaptogenic plant. Tri-terpenoid saponins and bacosides present in *Bacopa monnieri* are considered to be responsible for enhancing cognitive function (Russo & Borrelli, 2005), however the detailed mechanisms for its adaptogenic activity are yet to be explored. The standardized extract of *Bacopa monnieri* was reported earlier to have significant anxiolytic activity () and improve memory retention in Alzheimer's disease (Bhattacharya & Ghosal, 1998; Bhattacharya *et al.*, 1999) but the biochemical basis for the observed behavioural changes was not established. During stressful conditions, changes in monoamines -NA, DA and 5-HT, are well associated with transient behavioural aberrations in memory, learning and other mood disorders. Since *Bacopa monnieri* normalizes stress mediated transient deregulation of plasma corticosterone and monoamine changes in brain is one of the reasons for its adaptogenic activity (Rai *et al.*, 2003) and mild anxiolytic effects, respectively (Shanker & Singh, 2000). Deregulated function of monoamines is one of the principle reasons for memory dysfunction during stressful conditions (Rachel *et al.*, 2003)

Anti-cancer activity of the alcoholic extract (Elangovan *et al.*, 1995) and analgesic activity of bacosine, a tri-terpenoid isolated from the plant (Vohora *et al.*, 1997) have also been reported. Alkaloids, steroids, tri-terpenoids, hydrocarbons, flavanoids, amino acids and saponins were reported from the plant. Studies also indicated the protective effect of *Bacopa monnieri* extract on morphine induced brain mitochondrial enzyme activity. The dammarane tri-terpene glycosides bacoside A and bacoside B isolated from the plant have been shown to be responsible for the neuropharmacological activities of the plant. It has been found to be well tolerated and without any untoward reaction or side effects in regulatory pharmacological and toxicological studies. The LD50 of aqueous and alcoholic crude extracts of *Bacopa monnieri* in rats were 1000 mg and 15 g/Kg by intraperitoneal route, respectively (Martis et al., 1992). The aqueous crude extract given orally at a dose of 5 g/Kg did not show any toxicity. The LD50 of the alcoholic crude extract was 17 g/Kg given orally.

Animal behaviour is the bridge between the molecular and physiological aspects of biology and the ecological. Behaviour is the link between organisms and environment as well as between the nervous system and the ecosystem. Behaviour is one of the most important properties of animal life. Behaviour plays a critical role in biological adaptations. Behaviour is that part of an organism by which it interacts with its environment. Neuroethology, the integration of animal behaviour and the neurosciences, provides important frameworks for hypothesizing neural mechanisms. Careful behavioural data allow neurobiologists to narrow the scope of their studies and to focus on relevant input stimuli and attend to relevant responses. In many case the use of species specific natural stimuli has led to new insights about neural structure and function that contrast with results obtained using non-relevant stimuli.

Anxiety like behaviours in rats were measured using two pharmacologically well-validated exploration-based tests, elevated plus-maze (Komada *et al.*, 2008) and novel open field (Cryan & Holmes, 2005; Rodgers, 1997). The elevated plus maze test is one of the most popular tests of all currently available animal models of anxiety (Crawley, 2007). This test for anxiety-like behaviour has been used for screening and phenotyping transgenic and knockout mice (Horii *et al.*, 2008; Tsujimura *et al.*, 2008) and for drug discovery. The elevated plus maze test has a strong predictive validity for screening anxiolytic drugs (Mechiel & De Boer, 2003); anxiolytic drugs specifically increase, and anxiogenic drugs specifically decrease, the number of entries into the open arms and the time spent there. Depression-related behaviour was tested using a pharmacologically-validated test, the forced swim test (Rodgers, 1997; Olivier *et al.* 2008), sucrose consumption test and social interaction test (Sano *et al.*, 2008). Rotarod test has been previously been employed to assess the motor skills in rodents (Samad *et al.*, 2008).

The present work was carried out to investigate the alterations of the 5-HT$_{2C}$ and NMDA receptors in the brain regions of pilocarpine induced epileptic rats. The work focuses on the evaluation of the antiepileptic activity of extracts of *Bacopa monnieri in vivo* acting through 5-HT$_{2C}$ and NMDA receptors and the second messengers IP3, cGMP and cAMP. Gene expression studies using Real-time will be done to confirm receptor data. This will be confirmed by confocal microscopic studies using immunofluorescent antibodies to specific receptor subtypes. These molecular level changes will be confirmed with behavioural studies. These studies will help us to elucidate the functional role of 5-HT$_{2C}$ and NMDA receptors in epilepsy and the neuroprotective role of *Bacopa monnieri* through 5-HT$_{2C}$ and NMDA receptors during epilepsy which has immense therapeutic relevance in the management of epilepsy.

Materials and Methods

Chemicals used and their sources

Biochemicals used in the present study were purchased from Sigma Chemical Co., St. Louis, USA. All other reagents were of analytical grade purchased locally.

Biochemicals

Mesulergine, ethylene diamine tetra acetic acid (EDTA), Tris HCl, calcium chloride, atropine, Carbamazepine, Pilocarpine, and MK-801 were purchased from Sigma Chemical Co., St. Louis, USA. All other reagents were of analytical grade purchased locally. HPLC solvents were of HPLC grade obtained from SRL, India.and Sigma Chemical Co., St. Louis, USA.

Radiochemicals

$[N^6$-methyl-^{3}H] mesulergine (Sp. Activity 79.0 Ci/mmol) was purchased from Amersham Life Science, UK. (+)-[3-^{3}H] MK-801 (Sp. Activity 27.5 Ci/mmol) was purchased from Perkin Elmer Nen Life and Analytical Sciences, Boston, MA, USA. The [^{3}H] IP3, [^{3}H] cGMP and [^{3}H] cAMP Biotrak Assay Systems were purchased from G.E Healthcare UK Limited, UK.

Molecular Biology Chemicals

Tri-reagent kit was purchased from Sigma Chemical Co., St. Louis, USA. ABI PRISM High Capacity cDNA Archive kit, Primers and Taqman probes for Real-Time PCR were purchased from Applied Biosystems, Foster City, CA, USA. 5-HT$_{2C}$ (Rn00562748_m1), NMDA2b (Rn00561352_m1), mGlu5 (Rn00566628_m1) and GLAST (Rn00570130_m1) primers were used for the study.

Confocal Dyes

Immunofluorescent antibodies of 5-HT_{2C} was purchased from Neuromics, USA. Fluorescently labeled NMDA2b and mGlu5 receptor specific antibodies were obtained from Becton and Dickinson, USA. FITC and Rhodamine were purchased from Chemicon, USA.

Animals

Adult male Wistar rats of 250-300g body weight purchased from Amrita Institue of Medical Sciences, Cochin were used for all experiments. They were housed in separate cages under 12 hrs light and 12 hrs dark periods and were maintained on standard food pellets and water ad libitum.

Plant Material

Specimens of *Bacopa monnieri* were collected from Cochin University area. The plants were taxonomically identified and authenticated by Mr. K.P. Joseph, Head of the Dept. of Botany (Retd), St. Peter's College, Kolenchery and voucher specimens are deposited at the herbarium of the Centre for Neuroscience, Dept. of Biotechnology, Cochin University of Science and Technology, Cochin, Kerala (No. MNCB3).

Preparation of Bacopa monnieri Plant Extract

Crude whole plant extract was used to study the anti-epileptic effect in pilocarpine induced temporal lobe epilepsy. *Bacopa monnieri* plant extract was prepared by the procedure of Paulose *et al.*, (2008). Fresh, whole *Bacopa monnieri* plant (6–8 months old) was collected (in the month of March) and washed. Leaves, roots and stems of *Bacopa monnieri* plant were cut into small pieces and dried in shade. About 100 g fresh plant dried in shade yielded 15 g powder. Homogenate was extracted at required concentration (300 mg fresh plant/Kg body weight) by dissolving 450 mg of dried powder in 80 ml distilled water and used to study the anti-epileptic effect in pilocarpine induced temporal lobe epilepsy.

Epilepsy Induction

Adult male Wistar rats, weighing 250 to 300 g, were housed for 1 to 2 weeks before experiments were performed. Experimental animals were injected with pilocarpine (350 mg/Kg i.p.), preceded by 30 min with atropine (1 mg/Kg i.p.) to reduce peripheral pilocarpine effects. Within 20 to 40 min after the pilocarpine injection, essentially all of the animals developed *status epilepticus* (SE). Behavioural observation continued for 5 hrs after pilocarpine injection. Pilocarpine induced seizures were graded according to the Racine scale using stage 1-5: Stage 0- in which the rats showed no convulsion; stage 1- in which rats showed Facial Automatism; stage 2- Head nodding, stage 3- unilateral forelimb clonus, stage 4- bilateral forelimb clonus, stage- 5, rearing, falling and generalized convulsions. The occurrence of stage 3-5 was considered as one complete seizure. SE was allowed to continue for 1 hr and then control and experimental animals were treated with diazepam (4 mg/Kg i.p.). Animals recovered from this initial treatment within 2 to 3 days and were observed for the next 3 weeks. Animals were monitored by video recording and by clinical observation to evaluate the development of seizure discharge. Seizures were scored on a scale from 1 to 5, as used for the scoring of kindled seizures as described by Racine, (1972). Over 80% of the animals were found to have recurrent partial and generalized seizures after 3-4 weeks after the initial pilocarpine injection. No seizures were observed in control animals. 24 days after pilocarpine treatment, the rats were continuously video monitored for 72 hrs. The behaviour and seizures were captured with a CCD camera and a Pinnacle PCTV capturing software card and stored in the hard disk of the computer. One trained technician, blind to all experimental conditions, 58 viewed all videos. Seizure activity was rated as previously mentioned by Racine (1972). Seizures were assessed by viewing behavioural postures (i.e. lordosis, straight tail, jumping/ running, forelimb clonus and/or rearing during fast forward observation of the videos. Once a behavioural posture was observed the video was rewound to the beginning of the behaviour and examined at real-time speed.

Determination of Anti-Epileptic Potential of *Bacopa monnieri*

Experimental animals were divided into following groups
   a) Group 1 Control (given saline injection)
   b) Group 2 Epileptic
   c) Group 3 Control rats treated with *Bacopa monnieri*
   d) Group 4 Epileptic rats treated with *Bacopa monnieri*
   e) Group 5 Epileptic rats treated with Carbamazepine

Animal Groups

The rats were initially divided into two groups- Control and Epileptic. The epileptic group was injected with pilocarpine according to the previously established protocols as described earlier (Reas *et al.*, 2008). The control group received saline instead of pilocarpine. The epileptic group showed spontaneous recurrent seizures approximately 20 minutes after pilocarpine injection. Those rats that did not show spontaneous seizures after pilocarpine treatment were excluded form the study group. The rats were singly housed and maintained for 24 days with standard food and water *ad libitum* after pilocarpine treatment. After 24 days the rats were subjected continuous video monitoring for 72 hrs. The behaviour and seizures were observed. Those experimental rats that did not show seizures were excluded from the study group. The experimental group was again divided into four. The first group that did not receive the treatment was epileptic. Carbamazepine was given orally to the third group of epileptic rats (150 mg/ Kg body weight/day). Extract of *Bacopa monnieri* was given orally to the third and fourth group of epileptic rats in the dosage of 300 mg fresh plant/Kg body weight/ day for 15 days. After 15 days of treatment the rats were again subjected to continuous video monitoring for 72 hrs. The rats were sacrificed after the video observation.

Estimation of Blood Glucose

Blood glucose was estimated using Glucose estimation kit (Merck). The spectrophotometric method using glucose oxidase-peroxidase reactions is as follows:

Principle: Glucose oxidase (GOD) catalyses the oxidation of glucose in accordance with the following equation:

$$\text{Glucose} + O_2 + H_2O \xrightarrow{\text{(GOD)}} \text{Gluconic acid} + H_2O_2$$

$$H_2O_2 + \text{Phenol} + 4\text{- aminoantipyrene} \xrightarrow{\text{(PEROXIDASE)}} \text{Coloured complex} + H_2O$$

The hydrogen peroxide formed in this reaction reacts with 4-aminoantipyrine and 4-hydroxybenzoic acid in the presence of peroxidase (POD) to form N-(-4-antipyryl)-p-benzo quinoneimine. The addition of mutarotase accelerates the reactions. The amount of dye formed is proportional to the glucose concentration. The absorbance was read at 505nm in (Shimadzu UV-1700 pharmaSPEC) spectrophotometer.

Tissue preparation

Control and experimental rats were sacrificed by decapitation. The brain regions (cerebral cortex, cerebellum and brainstem) and body parts were dissected out quickly over ice according to the procedure of Glowinski & Iversen (1966). Hippocampus was dissected out quickly over ice according to the procedure of Heffner *et al.*, (1980). The tissues were stored at –80°C for various experiments. All animal care and procedures were in accordance with Institutional and National Institute of Health guidelines.

**Quantification of brain monoamines and their metabolites in the
experimental groups of rats.**

The monoamines were assayed according to the modified procedure of
Paulose *et al.*, (1988). The cerebral cortex, hippocampus, brain stem and
Cerebellum (CB) of experimental groups of rats was homogenised in 0.4N
perchloric acid. The homogenate was then centrifuged at 5000xg for 10 minutes
at 4°C in a Sigma 3K30 refrigerated centrifuge and the clear supernatant was
filtered through 0.22 µm HPLC grade filters and used for HPLC analysis.

5-hydroxy indole Acetic Acid (5-HIAA) and serotonin (5-HT) contents
were determined in high performance liquid chromatography (HPLC) with
electrochemical detector (ECD) (Waters, USA) fitted with CLC-ODS reverse
phase column of 5 µm particle size. The mobile phase consisted of 50mM sodium
phosphate dibasic, 0.03M citric acid, 0.1mM EDTA, 0.6mM sodium octyl
sulfonate, 15% methanol. The pH was adjusted to 3.25 with orthophosphoric acid,
filtered through 0.22 µm filter (Millipore) and degassed. A Waters model 515,
Milford, USA, pump was used to deliver the solvent at a rate of 1 ml/minute. The
neurotransmitters and their metabolites were identified by amperometric detection
using an electrochemical detector (Waters, model 2465) with a reduction potential
of +0.80 V. Twenty microlitre aliquots of the acidified supernatant were injected
into the system for quantification. The peaks were identified by relative retention
times compared with external standards and quantitatively estimated using an
integrator (Empower software) interfaced with the detector. Data from different
brain regions of the experimental and control rats were statistically analysed and
tabulated.

5-HT$_{2C}$ RECEPTOR BINDING STUDIES USING [^{3}H] RADIOLIGANDS IN THE BRAIN REGIONS OF CONTROL AND EXPERIMENTAL RATS

5-HT$_{2C}$ Receptor Binding Studies Using [^{3}H]mesulergine

5-HT$_{2C}$ receptor assay was done using [^{3}H] mesulergine in the synaptic membrane preparations of brain regions were done as previously described by Herrick-Davis *et al.*, (1999). Crude synaptic membrane preparation was suspended in 50 mM Tris-HCl buffer, pH 7.4 and used for assay. In the saturation binding experiments, assays were done using different concentrations i.e., 0.05nM-3nM of [^{3}H] mesulergine was incubated with and without excess of unlabelled 100µM 5-HT. Tubes were incubated at 25°C for 60 min. and filtered rapidly through GF/C filters (Whatman). The filters were washed quickly by three successive washing with 5.0 ml of ice cold 50mM Tris-HCl buffer, pH 7.4. Bound radioactivity was counted with cocktail-T in a Wallac 1409 liquid scintillation counter.

NMDA RECEPTOR BINDING STUDIES USING [^{3}H] RADIOLIGANDS IN THE BRAIN REGIONS OF CONTROL AND EXPERIMENTAL RATS

NMDA Receptor Binding Studies Using [^{3}H] MK-801

The membrane fractions were prepared by a modification of the method described by Hoffman *et al.*, (1996). Cerebral cortex was homogenized in a 0.32 M sucrose buffer solution containing 10 mM HEPES/1 mM EDTA buffer, pH 7.0. The homogenate was centrifuged at 1,000 × g for 10 min and the supernatant was centrifuged at 40,000 × g for 1 h. The pellet was resuspended and homogenized in 10 mM HEPES buffer containing 1.0 mM EDTA, pH 7.0 and centrifuged at 40,000 × g for 1 h. The final pellet was suspended in HEPES/EDTA buffer and stored at -80°C until binding assays were performed. The [^{3}H] MK-801 binding saturation assay was performed in a concentration range of 0.25 to 50 nM at 23°C in an assay medium containing 10 mM HEPES, pH 7.0, 200 - 250 µg of protein, 100 µM glycine and 100 µM glutamate. After 1 h of incubation, the reaction was stopped by filtration through GF/B filters and washed with HEPES buffer pH 7.0. Specific [³H] MK-801 binding was obtained by subtracting nonspecific binding in the presence of 100 μM unlabeled MK-801 from the total binding. Bound radioactivity was counted with cocktail-T in a Wallac 1409 a liquid scintillation counter

Protein determination

Protein was measured by the method of Lowry *et al.*, (1951) using bovine serum albumin as standard. The intensity of the purple blue colour formed was proportional to the amount of protein which was read in Spectrophotometer at 660nm.

ANALYSIS OF THE RECEPTOR BINDING DATA

Linear regression analysis for Scatchard plots

The data was analysed according to Scatchard (1949). The specific binding was determined by subtracting non-specific binding from the total. The binding parameters, maximal binding (B_{max}) and equilibrium dissociation constant (K_d), were derived by linear regression analysis by plotting the specific binding of the radioligand on X-axis and bound/free on Y-axis. The maximal binding is a measure of the total number of receptors present in the tissue and the equilibrium dissociation constant is the measure of the affinity of the receptors for the radioligand. The K_d is inversely related to receptor affinity.

GENE EXPRESSION STUDIES OF 5-HT$_{2C}$, NMDA2b, mGlu5 and GLAST RECEPTOR INDIFFERENT BRAIN REGIONS OF CONTROL AND EXPERIMENTAL RATS.

Preparation of RNA

RNA was isolated from the different brain regions (cerebral cortex, hippocampus, cerebellum and brainstem) of control and experimental rats using the Tri reagent from Sigma Aldrich.

Isolation of RNA

Tissue (25-50 mg) homogenates were made in 0.5 ml Tri Reagent and was centrifuged at 12,000xg for 10 minutes at 4^0C. The clear supernatant was transferred to a fresh tube and it was allowed to stand at room temperature for 5 minutes. 100µl of chloroform was added to it, mixed vigorously for 15 seconds and allowed to stand at room temperature for 15 minutes. The tubes were then centrifuged at 12,000xg for 15 minutes at 4°C. Three distinct phases appear after centrifugation. The bottom red organic phase contained protein, interphase contained DNA and a colourless upper aqueous phase contained RNA. The upper aqueous phase was transferred to a fresh tube and 250µl of isopropanol was added and the tubes were allowed to stand at room temperature for 10 minutes. The tubes were centrifuged at 12,000xg for 10 min at 4°C. RNA precipitate forms a pellet on the sides and bottom of the tube. The supernatants were removed and the RNA pellet was washed with 500µl of 75% ethanol, vortexed and centrifuged at 12,000xg for 5 min at 4°C. The pellets were semi dried and dissolved in minimum volume of DEPC-treated water. 2 µl of RNA was made up to 1 ml and absorbance were measured at 260nm and 280nm in spectrophotometer (Shimadzu UV-1700 pharmaSPEC). For pure RNA preparation the ratio of absorbance at 260/280 was $\geq$ 1.7. The concentration of RNA was calculated as one absorbance $_{260}$ = 42µg.

cDNA Synthesis

Total cDNA synthesis was performed using ABI PRISM cDNA Archive kit in 0.2ml microfuge tubes. The reaction mixture of 20µl contained 0.2µg total RNA, 10X RT buffer, 25X dNTP mixture, 10X Random primers, MultiScribe RT (50U/µl) and RNase free water. The cDNA synthesis reactions were carried out at 25^0C for 10 minutes and 37^0C for 2 hours using an Eppendorf Personal Cycler. The primers and probes were purchased from Applied Biosystems, Foster City, CA, USA designed using Primer Express Software Version (3.0).

Real -Time PCR Assay

Real Time PCR assays were performed in 96-well plates in a ABI 7300 Real Time PCR instrument (Applied Biosystems). To detect gene expression, a TaqMan quantitative 2-step reverse transcriptase "polymerase chain reaction (RT-PCR) was used to quantify mRNA levels. First-strand cDNA was synthesized with use of a TaqMan RT reagent kit, as recommended by the manufacturer. PCR analyses were conducted with gene-specific primers and fluorescently labeled TaqMan probe, designed by Applied Biosystems. Endogenous control, β-actin, was labelled with a reporter dye (VIC). All reagents were purchased from Applied Biosystems. The probes for specific gene of interest were labeled with FAM at the 5' end and a quencher (Minor Groove Binding Protein - MGB) at the 3' end. The Real-Time data were analyzed with Sequence Detection Systems software version 1.7. All reactions were performed in duplicate.

The TaqMan reaction mixture of 20µl contained 25ng of total RNA-derived cDNAs, 200nM each of the forward primer, reverse primer and PCR analyses were conducted with gene-specific primers and fluorescently labelled Taqman probes of 5-HT$_{2C}$ (Rn00562748_m1), NMDA2b (Rn00561352_m1), mGlu5 (Rn00566628_m1) and GLAST (Rn00570130_m1). Endogenous control (β-actin) was labeled with a reporter dye (VIC). 12.5µl of TaqMan 2X Universal PCR Master Mix was taken and the volume was made up with RNAse free water. Each run contained both negative (no template) and positive controls.

The thermocycling profile conditions were as follows:

50°C -- 2 minutes ---- Activation

95°C -- 10 minutes ---- Initial Denaturation

95°C -- 15 seconds ---- Denaturation   40 cycles

50°C -- 30 seconds --- Annealing

60°C -- 1 minutes --- Final Extension

Fluorescence signals measured during amplification were considered positive if the fluorescence intensity was 20-fold greater than the standard deviation of the baseline fluorescence. The $\Delta\Delta CT$ method of relative quantification was used to determine the fold change in expression. This was done by first normalizing the resulting threshold cycle (CT) values of the target mRNAs to the CT values of the internal control β-actin in the same samples ($\Delta CT = CT_{Target} - CT_{\beta\text{-actin}}$). It was further normalized with the control ($\Delta\Delta CT = \Delta CT - CT_{Control}$). The fold change in expression was then obtained ($2^{-\Delta\Delta CT}$).

IP3 CONTENT IN THE BRAIN REGIONS OF CONTROL AND EXPERIMENTAL RATS *IN VIVO*

Brain tissues – cerebral cortex, hippocampus, cerebellum and brainstem were homogenised in a polytron homogeniser in 50mM Tris-HCl buffer, pH.7.4, containing 1mM EDTA to obtain a 15% homogenate. The homogenate was then centrifuged at 40,000xg for 15 min. and the supernatant was transferred to fresh tubes for IP3 assay using [^{3}H]IP3 Biotrak Assay System kit.

Principle of the assay

The assay was based on competition between [^{3}H]IP3 and unlabelled IP3 in the standard or samples for binding to a binding protein prepared from bovine adrenal cortex. The bound IP3 was then separated from the free IP3 by centrifugation. The free IP3 in the supernatant was then discarded by simple decantation, leaving the bound fraction adhering to the tube. Measurement of the radioactivity in the tube enables the amount of unlabelled IP3 in the sample to be determined.

Assay Protocol

Standards, ranging from 0.19 to 25 pmoles/tube, [^{3}H]IP3 and binding protein were added together and the volume was made up to 100µl with assay buffer. Samples of appropriate concentration from experiments were used for the assay. The tubes were then vortexed and incubated on ice for 15 minutes and they were centrifuged at 2000 x g for 10 minutes at 4°C. The supernatant was aspirated out and the pellet was resuspended in water and incubated at room temperature for 10 minutes. The tubes were then vortexed and decanted immediately into scintillation vials. The radioactivity in the suspension was determined using liquid scintillation counter.

A standard curve was plotted with %B/Bo on the Y-axis and IP3 concentration (pmoles/tube) on the X-axis of a semi-log graph paper. $\%B/B_o$ was calculated as:

$$\frac{(\text{Standard or sample cpm} - \text{NSB cpm})}{(B_0 \text{ cpm} - \text{NSB cpm})} \times 100$$

NSB- non specific binding and B_0 - zero binding. IP3 concentration in the samples was determined by interpolation from the plotted standard curve.

cGMP CONTENT IN THE BRAIN REGIONS OF CONTROL AND EXPERIMENTAL RATS *IN VIVO*

Brain tissues - cerebral cortex, hippocampus, cerebellum and brainstem were homogenised in a polytron homogeniser with cold 50mM Tris-HCl buffer, pH 7.4, containing 1mM EDTA to obtain a 15% homogenate. The homogenate was then centrifuged at 40,000xg for 15 min and the supernatant was transferred to fresh tubes for cGMP assay using [^{3}H]cGMP Biotrak Assay System kit.

Principle of the assay

The assay is based on the competition between unlabelled cGMP and a fixed quantity of the [^{3}H]cGMP for binding to an antiserum, which has a high specificity and affinity for cGMP. The amount of [^{3}H]cGMP bound to the antiserum is inversely related to the amount of cGMP present in the assay sample. Measurement of the antibody bound radioactivity enables the amount of unlabelled cGMP in the sample to be calculated. Separation of the antibody bound cGMP from the unbound nucleotide was done by ammonium sulphate precipitation, followed by centrifugation. The precipitate which contains the antibody bound complex was resuspended in water and its activity was determined by liquid scintillation counting. The concentration of unlabelled cGMP in the sample was determined from a linear standard curve.

Assay Protocol

Standards, ranging from 0.5 to 4.0 pmoles/tube, and [^{3}H]cGMP were added together and the volume was made up to 100μl with assay buffer. Samples of appropriate concentration from experiments were used for the assay. The antiserum was added to all the assay tubes and then vortexed. The tubes were incubated for 90 minutes at 2 - 8°C. Ammonium sulphate was added to all tubes, mixed and allowed to stand for 5 minutes in ice bath. The tubes were centrifuged at 12000xg for 2 minutes at room temperature. The supernatant was aspirated out and the pellet was resuspended in water and decanted immediately into scintillation vials. The radioactivity in the suspension was determined using liquid scintillation counter.

A standard curve was plotted with Co/Cx on the Y-axis and cGMP concentration (pmoles/tube) on the X-axis of a linear graph paper. Co - the cpm bound in the absence of unlabelled cGMP; Cx - the cpm bound in the presence of standard/unknown cGMP. cGMP concentration in the samples was determined by interpolation from the plotted standard curve.

cAMP CONTENT IN THE BRAIN REGIONS OF CONTROL AND EXPERIMENTAL RATS *IN VIVO*

Brain tissues - cerebral cortex, hippocampus, cerebellum and brainstem were homogenised in a polytron homogeniser with cold 50mM Tris-HCl buffer, pH 7.4, containing 1mM EDTA to obtain a 15% homogenate. The homogenate was then centrifuged at 40,000 x g for 15min and the supernatant was transferred to fresh tubes for cAMP assay using [^{3}H]cAMP Biotrak Assay System kit.

Principle of the assay

cAMP assay kit was used. The assay is based on the competition between unlabelled cAMP and a fixed quantity of tritium labeled compound for binding to a protein which has a high specificity and affinity for cAMP. The amount of labeled protein -cAMP complex formed is inversely related to the amount of unlabelled cAMP present in the assay sample. Measurement of the protein-bound radioactivity enables the amount of unlabelled cAMP in the sample to be calculated.

Free [^{3}H] cAMP   Bound   [^{3}H]   cAMP-binding protein

$+$ Binding protein $=$ $+$

cAMP   cAMP-binding protein

Separation of the protein bound cAMP from unbound nucleotide was achieved by adsorption of the free nucleotide on to a coated charcoal followed by centrifugation. An aliquot of the supernatant is then removed for liquid scintillation counting. The concentration of unlabelled cAMP in the sample was then determined from a linear standard curve.

Assay Protocol

The tubes were placed on a water bath at 0°C. The assay mixture consisted of different concentrations of standard, [^{3}H]cAMP and binding protein in case of standards; buffer, [^{3}H]cAMP and binding protein for zero blank and unknown samples, [^{3}H]cAMP and binding protein for determination of unknown samples. The mixture was incubated at 2°C for 2h. Cold charcoal reagent was added to the tubes and the tubes were immediately centrifuged at 12,000 x g for 2min at 2°C. Aliquots of the supernatant was immediately transferred to scintillation vials and mixed with cocktail-T and counted in a liquid scintillation counter (Wallac, 1409).

C_o/C_x is plotted on the Y-axis against picomoles of inactive cAMP on the X- axis of a linear graph paper, where C_o is the counts per minute bound in the absence of unlabelled cAMP and C_x is the counts per minute bound in the presence of standard or unknown unlabelled cAMP. From the C_o/C_x value for the sample, the number of picomoles of unknown cAMP was calculated.

Elevated Plus Maze

The elevated plus-maze is a widely used animal model of anxiety that is based on two conflicting tendencies; the rodent's drive to explore a novel environment and it's aversion to heights and open spaces. Four arms were arranged in the shape of a cross. Two arms had side walls and an end wall ("closed arms") - the two other arms had no walls ("open arms"). The open arms were surrounded by small ledges to prevent the animal from falling from the maze. The maze was fastened to a light-weight support frame. Thus "anxious" animals spent most of the time in the closed arms while less anxious animals explored open areas longer. The control and experimental groups of rats were subjected to social interaction test during post- treatment period once daily for 15 days.

Rats were placed individually into the centre of elevated plus-maze consisting of two open arms (38L x 5W cm) and two closed arms (38L x 5W x 15H cm), with a central intersection (5cm x 5cm) elevated 50 cm above the floor. Behaviour was tested in a dimly lit room with a 40W bulb hung 60 cm above the central part of the maze. The investigator sitting approximately 2 metre apart from the apparatus observes and detects the movements of the rats for a total of 5 minutes. The experimental procedure was similar to that described by Pellow *et al.*, (1985). During the 5 minutes test period the following parameters were measured to analyze the behavioural changes of the experimental rats using elevated plus-maze: open arm entry, closed arm entry, percentage arm entry, total arm entry, time spent in open arm, time spent in closed arm, percentage of time spent in open arm, head dipping, stretched attend posture and grooming (Holmes & Rodgers, 1998). An entry was defined as entering with all four feet into one arm.

Rotarod Test

Rotarod has been used to evaluate motor coordination by testing the ability of rats to remain on revolving rod (Dunham & Miya, 1957). The control and experimental groups of rats were subjected to social interaction test during post- treatment period once daily for 15 days. The apparatus has a horizontal rough metal rod of 3 cm diameter attached to a motor with variable speed. This 70 cm long rod was divided into four sections by wooden partitions. The rod was placed at a height of 50 cm to discourage the animals to jump from the rotating rod. The rate of rotation was adjusted to allow the normal rats to stay on it for five minutes. Each rat was given five trials before the actual reading was taken. The readings were taken at 10, 15 and 25 rpm after 15 days of treatment in all groups of rats.

Social Interaction

The control and experimental groups of rats were subjected to social interaction test during post- treatment period once daily for 15 days. In the social interaction test, as previously (Millan *et al.* 2005), described by two unfamiliar, weight-matched rats receiving the same treatment were placed in opposite corners for 10 min into a brightly-lit chamber (30 × 30 × 60 cm; width, length and height, respectively) with floor covered with wood shavings. The total time spent in active social behaviour - allogrooming, sniffing the partner, crawling under and over, following was recorded, for each rat separately.

Forced Swim Test

The control and experimental groups of rats were subjected to forced swim test during post- treatment period once daily for 15 days as reported in Porsolt *et al.* (1977) and Millan *et al.* (2001). In short, cylindrical glass tanks (50 cm tall X18 cm diameter), filled to a depth of 30 cm with 22 (±1) °C water and were used in the forced swimming test. Testing consisted of two phases, the induction phase and the test phase. During the induction phase animals were placed in the water for 15 min. After 24 h the rats are placed in the same tanks for

5 min. The movements of the rats were videotaped for off-line measurement of the duration of immobility (seconds). The behavioural variable 'immobility' was defined as follows: making no movements for at least 2 seconds or making only those movements that were necessary to keep the nose above the water. The rats were allowed to slightly move their forepaws or support themselves by pressing their paws against the wall of the cylinder. Active climbing, diving and swimming along the wall were scored as mobility and the time taken was recorded in seconds.

Confocal Studies

Control and experimental rats were deeply anesthetized with ether. The rat was transcardially perfused with PBS (pH- 7.4) followed by 4% paraformaldehyde in PBS (Chen *et al.*, 2007). After perfusion the brains were dissected and immersion fixed in 4% paraformaldehyde for 1 hr and then equilibrated with 30% sucrose solution in PBS (0.1 M). 40 µm sections were cut using Cryostat (Leica, CM1510 S). The sections were treated with PBST (PBS in 0.05% Triton X-100) for 20 min. Brain slices were were incubated overnight at 4 °C with either rat primary antibody for 5-HT$_{2C}$ (No: RA24505 Neuromics, diluted in PBST at 1: 500 dilution), NMDA2b (No: 610416 BD Biosciences, diluted in PBST at 1: 500 dilution), mGlu$_5$ (No: AB7130F, Chemicon, diluted in PBST at 1: 500 dilution) (polyclonal or monoclonal). After overnight incubation, the brain slices were rinsed with PBST and then incubated with appropriate secondary antibody of either FITC (No: AB7130F, Chemicon, diluted in PBST at 1: 1000 dilution) or Rhodamine dye (No:AP307R Chemicon, diluted in PBST at 1: 1000 dilution). The sections were observed and photographed using confocal imaging system (Leica SP 5).

STATISTICS

Statistical evaluations were done by ANOVA using InStat (Ver.2.04a) computer programme. Linear regression Scatchard plots were made using SIGMA PLOT (Ver 2.03). Sigma Plot software (version 2.0, Jandel GmbH,

Erkrath, Germany). Competitive binding data were analysed using non-linear regression curve-fitting procedure (GraphPad PRISM^{TM}, San Diego, USA). Empower software were used for HPLC analysis. Relative Quantification Software was used for analyzing Real-Time PCR results.

Results

Body weight, feed intake, water consumption and blood glucose level in control and experimental groups of rats

There was a significant reduction ($p<0.001$) in the body weight of epileptic rats compared to control rats and *Bacopa monnieri* treated control rats on 30th and 45th day of experiment. The body weight of *Bacopa monnieri* and carbamazepine treated epileptic rats reversed ($p<0.001$) to control on 30th and 45th day of experiment (Table- 1). There is a significant decrease ($p<0.001$) in the feed intake and water consumption of epileptic rats on 30th and 45th day of experiment compared to control rats and *Bacopa monnieri* treated control rats. Both *Bacopa monnieri* and carbamazepine treatment to epileptic rats significantly increased the feed intake and water consumption on 30th ($p<0.05$) and 45th ($p<0.001$) day of experiment (Table 2, 3). There was no significant change in the blood glucose level in the control and experimental groups of rats (Table- 4).

5-HT and 5-HIAA content (nmoles/g wet wt.) in the cerebral cortex of control and experimental groups of rats

5-HT content in the cerebral cortex showed a significant decrease ($p<0.001$) in epileptic rats compared to control rats and *Bacopa monnieri* treated control rats. *Bacopa monnieri* ($p<0.01$) and carbamazepine ($p<0.05$) treatment to epileptic rats significantly increased the 5-HT contents near to control. 5-HIAA content was significantly increased ($p<0.01$) in epileptic rats compared to control rats and *Bacopa monnieri* treated control rats. Both *Bacopa monnieri* ($p<0.01$) and carbamazepine ($p<0.05$) treatment to epileptic rats significantly decreased the 5-HIAA content to control. 5-HT/5-HIAA ratio showed a significant decrease ($p<0.001$) in the epileptic rats compared to control rats and *Bacopa monnieri* treated control rats. Treatment with

Bacopa monnieri (p<0.01) to epileptic rats significantly reversed the 5-HT/5-HIAA ratio towards control. Treatment with carbamazepine (p<0.05) to epileptic rats showed no significant change in the 5-HT/5-HIAA compared to epileptic rats (Table- 5).

5-HT and 5-HIAA content (nmoles/g wet wt.) in the hippocampus of control and experimental groups of rats

5-HT content in the hippocampus showed a significant decrease (p<0.01) in epileptic rats compared to control rats and *Bacopa monnieri* treated control rats. *Bacopa monnieri* (p<0.01) and carbamazepine (p<0.05) treatment to epileptic rats significantly increased the 5-HT contents near to control. 5-HIAA content was significantly increased in epileptic rats (p<0.001) and carbamazepine treated epileptic rats (p<0.001) compared to both control rats and *Bacopa monnieri* treated control rats. Only *Bacopa monnieri* (p<0.01) treatment to epileptic rats significantly decreased the 5-HIAA content to control. 5-HT/5-HIAA ratio showed no significant change in the hippocampus of control and experimental groups of rats (Table- 6).

5-HT and 5-HIAA content (nmoles/g wet wt.) in the cerebellum of control and experimental groups of rats

5-HT content in the cerebellum showed a significant decrease (p<0.001) in epileptic rats compared to control rats and *Bacopa monnieri* treated control rats. *Bacopa monnieri* (p<0.01) and carbamazepine (p<0.01) treatment to epileptic rats significantly increased the 5-HT contents near to control. 5-HIAA content was significantly increased in epileptic rats (p<0.001) and carbamazepine treated epileptic rats (p<0.05) compared to both control rats and *Bacopa monnieri* treated control rats. Only *Bacopa monnieri* (p<0.01) treatment to epileptic rats significantly decreased the 5-HIAA content to control. 5-HT/5-HIAA ratio showed a significant decrease (p<0.001) in the epileptic rats and carbamazepine treated epileptic rats (p<0.05) compared to control rats and *Bacopa monnieri* treated control rats. Treatments with

Bacopa monnieri (p<0.01) to epileptic rats significantly reversed the 5-HT/5-HIAA ratio towards control (Table- 7).

5-HT and 5-HIAA content (nmoles/g wet wt.) in the brainstem of control and experimental groups of rats

5-HT content in the brainstem showed a significant decrease (p<0.001) in epileptic rats compared to control rats and *Bacopa monnieri* treated control rats. *Bacopa monnieri* (p<0.05) and carbamazepine (p<0.01) treatment to epileptic rats significantly increased the 5-HT contents near to control. 5-HIAA content was significantly increased in epileptic rats (p<0.05) and carbamazepine treated epileptic rats (p<0.05) compared to both control rats and *Bacopa monnieri* treated control rats. Only *Bacopa monnieri* (p<0.05) treatment to epileptic rats significantly decreased the 5-HIAA content to control. 5-HT/5-HIAA ratio showed no significant change in the brainstem of control and experimental groups of rats (Table- 8).

BRAIN 5-HT$_{2C}$ RECEPTOR ALTERATIONS IN THE CONTROL AND EXPERIMENTAL GROUPS OF RATS

CEREBRAL CORTEX

Scatchard analysis using [^{3}H]mesulergine against mesulergine

Scatchard analysis of [^{3}H]mesulergine against mesulergine in cerebral cortex showed a significant increase (p<0.001) in B_{max} and K_d (p<0.01) of epileptic group compared to control rats and *Bacopa monnieri* treated control rats. Treatments with *Bacopa monnieri* and carbamazepine significantly reversed (p<0.001) the B_{max} to near control. K_d showed a significant decrease (p<0.01) in both *Bacopa monnieri* and carbamazepine treated groups compared to epileptic rats (Fig. 1; Table- 9).

Real-Time PCR analysis of 5-HT$_{2C}$ Receptors

The gene expression studies by Real-Time PCR analysis showed that 5-HT$_{2C}$ receptor mRNA in cerebral cortex was significantly (p<0.001) up regulated in epileptic group compared to control and *Bacopa monnieri* treated control rats. *Bacopa monnieri* and carbamazepine administration to epileptic rats significantly (p<0.01) reversed the up regulation compared to epileptic rats (Fig. 2; Table- 10).

HIPPOCAMPUS

Scatchard analysis using [^{3}H]mesulergine against mesulergine

Scatchard analysis of [^{3}H]mesulergine against mesulergine in hippocampus showed a significant increase (p<0.001) in B$_{max}$ and K$_d$ of epileptic group compared to control rats and *Bacopa monnieri* treated control rats. Treatments with *Bacopa monnieri* and carbamazepine significantly reversed (p<0.001) the B$_{max}$ to near control. K$_d$ showed a significant decrease in both *Bacopa monnieri* (p<0.01) and carbamazepine (p<0.001) treated groups compared to epileptic groups (Fig. 3; Table- 11).

Real-Time PCR analysis of 5-HT$_{2C}$ Receptors

The gene expression studies by Real-Time PCR analysis showed that 5-HT$_{2C}$ receptor mRNA in hippocampus was significantly (p<0.001) up regulated in epileptic group compared to control and *Bacopa monnieri* treated control rats. *Bacopa monnieri* and carbamazepine administration to epileptic rats significantly (p<0.01) reversed the up regulation to control (Fig. 4; Table- 12).

CEREBELLUM

Scatchard analysis using [^{3}H]mesulergine against mesulergine

Scatchard analysis of [^{3}H]mesulergine against mesulergine in cerebellum showed a significant decrease in B$_{max}$ (p<0.001) and K$_d$ (p<0.01) of epileptic group compared to control rats and *Bacopa monnieri* treated control rats. Treatments with *Bacopa monnieri* and carbamazepine significantly reversed ($p<0.001$) the B_{max} to near control. K_d showed a significant increase ($p<0.01$) in both *Bacopa monnieri* and carbamazepine treated groups compared to epileptic groups (Fig. 5; Table- 13).

Real-Time PCR analysis of 5-HT$_{2C}$ Receptors

The gene expression studies by Real-Time PCR analysis showed that 5-HT$_{2C}$ receptor mRNA in cerebellum was significantly ($p<0.001$) down regulated in epileptic group compared to control and *Bacopa monnieri* treated control rats. *Bacopa monnieri* and carbamazepine administration to epileptic rats significantly ($p<0.01$) reversed the down regulation to control level (Fig. 6; Table- 14).

BRAINSTEM

Scatchard analysis using [^{3}H]mesulergine against mesulergine

Scatchard analysis of [^{3}H]mesulergine against mesulergine in brainstem showed a significant decrease in B_{max} ($p<0.001$) of epileptic group compared to control rats and *Bacopa monnieri* treated control rats. Treatments with *Bacopa monnieri* and carbamazepine significantly reversed ($p<0.001$) the B_{max} to near control. There was no significant change in K_d of control and experimental groups of rats. (Fig. 7; Table- 15).

Real-Time PCR analysis of 5-HT$_{2C}$ Receptors

The gene expression studies by Real-Time PCR analysis showed that 5-HT$_{2C}$ receptor mRNA in brainstem was significantly ($p<0.001$) down regulated in epileptic group compared to control and *Bacopa monnieri* treated control rats. *Bacopa monnieri* and carbamazepine administration to epileptic rats significantly ($p<0.01$) reversed the down regulation to control level (Fig. 8; Table- 16).

BRAIN NMDA RECEPTOR ALTERATIONS IN THE CONTROL AND EXPERIMENTAL GROUPS OF RATS

CEREBRAL CORTEX

Scatchard analysis using [^{3}H]MK-801 against MK-801

Scatchard analysis of [^{3}H]MK-801 against MK-801 in cerebral cortex showed a significant decrease in B_{max}($p<0.001$) and of epileptic rats compared to control and *Bacopa monnieri* treated control rats. *Bacopa monnieri* ($p<0.001$) and carbamazepine ($p<0.001$) treatment to epileptic rats significantly reversed alterations in B_{max} to near control level (Fig. 9; Table- 17). There was no significant change in K_d in control and experimental rats.

Real-Time PCR analysis of NMDA2b Receptors

Real-Time PCR analysis showed that the NMDA2b receptor mRNA significantly decreased ($p<0.001$) in epileptic condition when compared to control and *Bacopa monnieri* treated control rats. *Bacopa monnieri* and carbamazepine treatment to epileptic rats significantly reversed ($p<0.01$) NMDA2b receptor mRNA alteration to near control (Fig. 10; Table- 18).

Real-Time PCR analysis of mGLU5 Receptors

The mGlu5 receptor mRNA was significantly increased ($p<0.001$) in epileptic condition compared to control and *Bacopa monnieri* treated control rats. *Bacopa monnieri* and carbamazepine treatment to epileptic rats significantly reversed ($p<0.001$) mGlu5 receptor mRNA alteration to near control (Fig. 11; Table- 19).

Real-Time PCR analysis of GLAST

The GLAST mRNA was significantly increased ($p<0.01$) in epileptic condition compared to control and *Bacopa monnieri* treated control rats. *Bacopa monnieri* and carbamazepine treatment to epileptic rats significantly reversed (p<0.01) the up regulation of GLAST mRNA compared to epileptic rats (Fig. 12; Table- 20).

HIPPOCAMPUS

Scatchard analysis using [^{3}H]MK-801 against MK-801

Scatchard analysis of [^{3}H]MK-801 against MK-801 in hippocampus showed a significant decrease in B_{max}(p<0.001) and in K_d (p<0.01) of epileptic rats compared to control and *Bacopa monnieri* treated control rats. *Bacopa monnieri* (p<0.01) and carbamazepine (p<0.001) treatment to epileptic rats significantly reversed alterations in B_{max} to near control level. *Bacopa monnieri* (p<0.05) treatment to epileptic rats significantly reversed alterations in K_d to near control level. Carbamzepine treatment to epileptic rats showed no significant change in K_d when compared to epileptic rats. (Fig 13; Table- 21).

Real-Time PCR analysis of NMDA2b Receptors

Real-Time-PCR analysis showed that the NMDA2b receptor mRNA in hippocampus significantly down regulated (p<0.001) in epileptic rats when compared to control *Bacopa monnieri* treated control rats. *Bacopa monnieri* (p<0.01) and carbamazepine treatment (p<0.001) to epileptic rats increased $NMDA_{2b}$ receptor mRNA to near control (Fig. 14; Table- 22).

Real-Time PCR analysis of mGLU5 Receptors

The mGlu5 receptor mRNA in hippocampus was significantly increased (p<0.001) in epileptic condition compared to control and *Bacopa monnieri* treated control rats. *Bacopa monnieri* (p<0.001) and carbamazepine treatment (p<0.01) to epileptic rats significantly reversed mGlu5 receptor mRNA alteration to near control (Fig. 15; Table- 23).

Real-Time PCR analysis of GLAST

The GLAST mRNA in hippocampus was significantly up regulated ($p<0.001$) in epileptic condition compared to control and *Bacopa monnieri* treated control rats. *Bacopa monnieri* ($p<0.01$) and carbamazepine treatment ($p<0.001$) to epileptic rats significantly reversed GLAST mRNA alteration to near control (Fig. 16; Table- 24).

CEREBELLUM

Scatchard analysis using [^{3}H]MK-801 against MK-801

Scatchard analysis of [^{3}H] MK-801 against MK-801 in cerebellum showed a significant increase in B_{max} ($p<0.001$) and K_d ($p<0.01$) of epileptic rats compared to control and *Bacopa monnieri* treated control rats. *Bacopa monnieri* ($p<0.001$) and carbamazepine ($p<0.001$) treatment to epileptic rats significantly reversed alterations in B_{max} to near control level (Fig. 17; Table- 25). There was no significant change in the K_d of both the treatment groups compared to control.

Real-Time PCR analysis of NMDA2b Receptors

Real Time-PCR analysis showed that the NMDA2b receptor mRNA in cerebellum significantly up regulated ($p<0.001$) in epileptic rats when compared to control *Bacopa monnieri* treated control rats. *Bacopa monnieri* and carbamazepine treatment to epileptic rats significantly decreased ($p<0.01$) NMDA2b receptor mRNA to near control (Fig. 18; Table- 26).

Real-Time PCR analysis of mGLU5 Receptors

The mGlu5 receptor mRNA was significantly up regulated ($p<0.001$) in cerebellum of epileptic rats compared to control and *Bacopa monnieri* treated control rats. Treatment with *Bacopa monnieri* ($p<0.001$) and carbamazepine treatment ($p<0.01$) to epileptic rats significantly reversed mGlu5 receptor mRNA alteration to near control (Fig. 19; Table- 27).

Real-Time PCR analysis of GLAST

The GLAST mRNA was significantly down regulated (p<0.001) in cerebellum of epileptic rats compared to control and *Bacopa monnieri* treated control rats. *Bacopa monnieri* (p<0.01) and carbamazepine (p<0.001) treatment to epileptic rats significantly reversed GLAST mRNA alteration to near control (Fig. 20; Table-28).

BRAINSTEM

Scatchard analysis using [^{3}H]MK-801 against MK-801

Scatchard analysis of [^{3}H]MK-801 against MK-801 showed a significant increase in B_{max} (p<0.001) and K_d (p<0.01) in brainstem of epileptic rats compared to control and *Bacopa monnieri* treated control rats. *Bacopa monnieri* and carbamazepine treatment to epileptic rats significantly reversed (p<0.001) NMDA receptor B_{max} alterations to near control. *Bacopa monnieri* (p<0.01) and carbamazepine (p<0.01) treatment to epileptic rats significantly reversed alterations in K_d to near control level (Fig. 21; Table- 29).

Real-Time PCR analysis of NMDA2b Receptors

Real Time-PCR analysis showed that the NMDA2b receptor mRNA in brainstem significantly up regulated (p<0.001) in epileptic rats when compared to control *Bacopa monnieri* treated control rats. *Bacopa monnieri* and carbamazepine treatment to epileptic rats significantly reversed (p<0.01) NMDA2b receptor mRNA to near control (Fig. 22; Table- 30).

Real-Time PCR analysis of mGLU5 Receptors

The mGlu5 receptor mRNA was significantly up regulated (p<0.001) in brainstem of epileptic rats compared to control and *Bacopa monnieri* treated control rats. Treatment with *Bacopa monnieri* (p<0.001) and carbamazepine (p<0.01) treatment to epileptic rats significantly reversed mGlu5 receptor mRNA alteration to near control (Fig. 23; Table- 31).

Real-Time PCR analysis of GLAST

The GLAST mRNA was significantly up regulated ($p < 0.001$) in brainstem of epileptic rats compared to control and *Bacopa monnieri* treated control rats. *Bacopa monnieri* and carbamazepine treatment to epileptic rats significantly reversed ($p < 0.01$) the GLAST mRNA alteration to near control (Fig. 24; Table- 32).

IP3 content in the cerebral cortex of control and experimental groups of rats

The IP3 content in the cerebral cortex was significantly increased ($p < 0.001$) in epileptic condition compared to control and *Bacopa monnieri* treated control rats. *Bacopa monnieri* ($p < 0.01$) and carbamazepine ($p < 0.05$) treatment to epileptic rats significantly reversed IP3 content alteration to near control level (Fig. 25; Table- 33).

IP3 content in the hippocampus of control and experimental groups of rats

The IP3 content in the hippocampus was significantly increased ($p < 0.001$) in epileptic condition compared to control and *Bacopa monnieri* treated control rats. *Bacopa monnieri* ($p < 0.01$) and carbamazepine ($p < 0.01$) treatment to epileptic rats significantly reversed IP3 content alteration to near control level (Fig. 26; Table- 34).

IP3 content in the cerebellum of control and experimental groups of rats

The IP3 content in the cerebellum was significantly decreased ($p < 0.001$) in epileptic condition compared to control and *Bacopa monnieri* treated control rats. *Bacopa monnieri* ($p < 0.01$) and carbamazepine ($p < 0.01$) treatment to epileptic rats significantly reversed IP3 content alteration to near control level (Fig. 27; Table- 35).

IP3 content in the brainstem of control and experimental groups of rats

The IP3 content in the brainstem was significantly increased ($p<0.001$) in epileptic condition compared to control and *Bacopa monnieri* treated control rats. *Bacopa monnieri* ($p<0.01$) and carbamazepine ($p<0.05$) treatment to epileptic rats significantly reversed IP3 content alteration to near control level (Fig. 28; Table- 36).

cGMP content in the cerebral cortex of control and experimental groups of rats

The cGMP content in the cerebral cortex was significantly decreased ($p<0.01$) in epileptic condition compared to control and *Bacopa monnieri* treated control rats. *Bacopa monnieri* and carbamazepine treatment to epileptic rats significantly reversed ($p<0.01$) the cGMP content alteration to near control level (Fig. 29; Table- 37).

cGMP content in the hippocampus of control and experimental groups of rats

The cGMP content in the hippocampus was significantly increased ($p<0.001$) in epileptic condition compared to control and *Bacopa monnieri* treated control rats. *Bacopa monnieri* ($p<0.01$) and carbamazepine ($p<0.01$) treatment to epileptic rats significantly reversed cGMP content alteration to near control level (Fig. 30; Table- 38).

cGMP content in the cerebellum of control and experimental groups of rats

The cGMP content in the cerebellum was significantly increased ($p<0.001$) in epileptic condition compared to control and *Bacopa monnieri* treated control rats. *Bacopa monnieri* ($p<0.01$) and carbamazepine ($p<0.05$) treatment to epileptic rats significantly reversed cGMP content alteration to near control level (Fig. 31; Table- 39).

cGMP content in the brainstem of control and experimental groups of rats

The cGMP content in the brainstem was significantly increased (p<0.001) in epileptic condition compared to control and *Bacopa monnieri* treated control rats. *Bacopa monnieri* (p<0.01) and carbamazepine (p<0.05) treatment to epileptic rats significantly reversed cGMP content alteration to near control level (Fig. 32; Table-40).

cAMP content in the cerebral cortex of control and experimental groups of rats

The cAMP content in the cerebral cortex was significantly increased (p<0.001) in epileptic rats compared to control and *Bacopa monnieri* treated control rats. *Bacopa monnieri* (p<0.001) and carbamazepine (p<0.01) treatment to epileptic rats significantly reversed cAMP content alteration to near control level (Fig. 33; Table- 41).

cAMP content in the hippocampus of control and experimental groups of rats

The cAMP content in the hippocampus was significantly increased (p<0.001) in epileptic condition compared to control and *Bacopa monnieri* treated control rats. *Bacopa monnieri* (p<0.01) and carbamazepine (p<0.05) treatment to epileptic rats significantly reversed cAMP content alteration to near control level (Fig. 34; Table-42).

cAMP content in the cerebellum of control and experimental groups of rats

The cAMP content in the cerebellum was significantly decreased (p<0.001) in epileptic condition compared to control and *Bacopa monnieri* treated control rats. *Bacopa monnieri* (p<0.01) and carbamazepine (p<0.01) treatment to epileptic rats significantly reversed cAMP content alteration to near control level (Fig. 35; Table-43).

cAMP content in the brainstem of control and experimental groups of rats

cAMP content in the brainstem was significantly decreased ($p<0.001$) in epileptic condition compared to control and *Bacopa monnieri* treated control rats. *Bacopa monnieri* ($p<0.001$) and carbamazepine ($p<0.001$) treatment to epileptic rats significantly reversed cAMP content alteration to near control level (Fig. 36; Table-44).

Rotarod Performance of control and experimental groups of rats

Rotarod experiment showed a significant decrease at 10 revolutions per minute (rpm) ($p<0.01$), 15 rpm ($p<0.001$) and 25 rpm ($p<0.001$) in the retention time on the rotating rod in epileptic group compared to control. *Bacopa monnieri* treatment to epileptic rats significantly reversed the retention time near to control at 10($p<0.01$), 15 ($p<0.01$) and 25 ($p<0.05$) rpm. Carbamazepine treatment to epileptic rats significantly reversed the retention time near to control at 10($p<0.01$), 15 ($p<0.001$) and 25 ($p<0.05$) rpm (Fig. 37; Table- 45).

Elevated Plus Maze Test in the control and experimental Rats

Behavioural response of control and experimental rats in open and closed arm entry (counts/5 minutes) in elevated plus maze test

The epileptic rats showed a significant increase in the number of entries made into open arm ($p<0.001$), closed arm ($p<0.01$) and total arm entry ($p<0.001$), compared to control and *Bacopa monnieri* treatment. *Bacopa monnieri* treatment to epileptic rats reversed the number of entries into open arm ($p<0.01$) closed arm ($p<0.05$) and total arm entry ($p<0.001$) to near control. Carbamazepine to epileptic rats treatment significantly decreased ($p<0.05$) the number of entries into open arm to near control (Table- 46).

Behavioural response of control and experimental rats in time spent (seconds/5 minutes) in open and closed arms in elevated plus maze test

There was a significant increase in time spent in the closed arm (p<0.001) and decrease (p<0.001) in the time spent in the open arm by epileptic rats compared to control and *Bacopa monnieri* treated control rats. There was significant increase in the time spent in the open arm by *Bacopa monnieri* (p<0.01) and carbamazepine (p<0.05) treated epileptic rats to near control. *Bacopa monnieri* and carbamazepine treatments to epileptic rats caused significant decrease (p<0.01) in time spent in the closed arm near to near control rats (Table- 47).

Percentage of time spent in open arm showed a significant decrease in epileptic (p<0.001) rats compared to control. *Bacopa monnieri* and carbamazepine treatments to epileptic rats caused significant increase (p<0.01) in time spent in the closed arm near to near control rats and *Bacopa monnieri* treated control rats (Table- 47).

Behavioural response of control and experimental rats in head dipping attempts, stretched attend posture and grooming attempts in elevated plus- maze test

There was a significant decrease in head dipping (p<0.01), stretched attend posture (p<0.001) and grooming attempts (p<0.001) in epileptic rats compared to control and *Bacopa monnieri* treated control rats. *Bacopa monnieri* and carbamazepine treatment to epileptic rats caused a significant increase (p<0.05) in head dipping attempt, stretched attend posture and grooming attempts to control (Table- 48).

Social Interaction Test in the control and experimental rats

Behavioral response of control and experimental rats at allogrooming, sniffing, aggressive attacks and following the partner in Social Interaction Test (Counts/10 minutes)

There was a significant decrease in the attempts in allogrooming ($p<0.001$), sniffing ($p<0.01$) and following ($p<0.05$) the partner by epileptic rats compared to control and *Bacopa monnieri* treated control rats. *Bacopa monnieri* treatment to epileptic rats caused a significant increase in the attempts at allogrooming ($p<0.05$), sniffing ($p<0.05$) and following ($p<0.01$) near to control rats. Carbamazepine treatment to epileptic rats caused a significant increase in the attempts at allogrooming ($p<0.05$), sniffing ($p<0.05$) and following ($p<0.01$) near to control rats. No aggressive attacks were observed in control and experimental groups of rats (Table- 49).

Behavioral response of control and experimental rats in time spent in social interaction test (seconds/10 minutes)

There was a significant decrease ($p<0.001$) in total time spent in social interaction and increase in time spent without social interaction ($p<0.001$) by epileptic rats compared to control and *Bacopa monnieri* treated control rats. *Bacopa monnieri* ($p<0.01$) and carbamazepine ($p<0.001$) treatment to epileptic rats caused a significant increase in the time spent social interaction compared to epileptic rats. *Bacopa monnieri* ($p<0.01$) and carbamazepine ($p<0.001$) treatment to epileptic rats significantly decreased the time spent without social interaction compared to epileptic rats (Table- 50).

Behavioural response of control and experimental rats in Forced Swim Test

There was a significant increase ($p<0.001$) in the immobility period and significant decrease ($p<0.001$) in mobile period spent in forced swim test by epileptic rats compared to control and *Bacopa monnieri* treated control rats. *Bacopa monnieri* and carbamazepine treatment to epileptic rats caused a significant increase (p<0.01) in the mobile period compared to epileptic rats. *Bacopa monnieri* (p<0.01) and carbamazepine (p<0.001) treatment to epileptic rats also significantly decreased the immobile period compared to epileptic rats (Table- 51).

CONFOCAL STUDIES

Cerebral Cortex

5-HT$_{2C}$ receptor antibody staining in control and experimental groups of rats

The 5-HT$_{2C}$ receptor antibody staining in the cerebral cortex showed an increase in the 5-HT$_{2C}$ receptor in epileptic rat compared to control and *Bacopa monnieri* treated control rats. *Bacopa monnieri* and carbamazepine treated epileptic rats showed a reversal of the increase in 5-HT$_{2C}$ receptor staining in the cerebral cortex compared to epileptic rats. (Fig. 38; Table- 52).

NMDA2b receptor antibody staining in control and experimental groups of rats

The NMDA2b receptor antibody staining in the cerebral cortex showed a decrease in the NMDA2b receptor in epileptic rat compared to control and *Bacopa monnieri* treated control rats. *Bacopa monnieri* and carbamazepine treated epileptic rats showed a reversal in decreased NMDA2b receptor staining in the cerebral cortex compared to epileptic rats. (Fig. 39; Table- 53).

mGlu5 receptor antibody staining in control and experimental groups of rats

The mGlu5 receptor antibody staining in the cerebral cortex showed an increase in the 5-HT$_{2C}$ receptor in epileptic rat compared to control and *Bacopa monnieri* treated control rats. *Bacopa monnieri* and carbamazepine treated epileptic rats showed a reversal of the mGlu5 receptor staining in the cerebral cortex compared to epileptic rats. (Fig. 40; Table- 54).

Cerebellum

5-HT$_{2C}$ receptor antibody staining in control and experimental groups of rats

The 5-HT$_{2C}$ receptor antibody staining in the cerebellum showed an increase in the 5-HT$_{2C}$ receptor in epileptic rat compared to control and *Bacopa monnieri* treated control rats. *Bacopa monnieri* and carbamazepine treated epileptic rats showed a reversal in increased 5-HT$_{2C}$ receptor staining in the cerebral cortex compared to epileptic rats. (Fig. 41; Table- 55).

NMDA2b receptor antibody staining in control and experimental groups of rats

The NMDA2b receptor antibody staining in the cerebellum showed a decrease in the NMDA2b receptor in epileptic rat compared to control and *Bacopa monnieri* treated control rats. *Bacopa monnieri* and carbamazepine treated epileptic rats showed a reversal in decreased NMDA2b receptor staining in the cerebral cortex compared to epileptic rats. (Fig. 42; Table- 56).

mGlu5 receptor antibody staining in control and experimental groups of rats

The mGlu5 receptor antibody staining in the cerebellum showed an increase in the 5-HT$_{2C}$ receptor in epileptic rat compared to control and *Bacopa monnieri* treated control rats. *Bacopa monnieri* and carbamazepine treated epileptic rats showed a reversal in increased mGlu5 receptor staining in the cerebral cortex compared to epileptic rats. (Fig. 43; Table- 57).

Discussion

Epilepsy, a common neurological disorder characterized by recurrent spontaneous seizures, is considered to be a major health problem that affects approximately one to two percent of the population worldwide. The epileptogenesis is a dynamic process with major modifications taking place at multiple levels, which include synaptic plasticity, aberrant reorganization of the neuronal circuitry, alterations in interneuron number and function and changes in dentate neurogenesis. The latency period found between the initial precipitating insult and the development of chronic epilepsy offers a useful window for application of promising neuroprotective strategies. On basis of behavioural, electrophysiological and histopathological findings obtained with different protocols and by comparing mortality rates, onset of spontaneous recurrent seizures (SRSs), neuronal damage, and network reorganization, pilocarpine model is considered as a valuable tool to investigate the mechanisms involved in TLE.

We observed a decrease in the body weight of epileptic rats compared to control and *Bacopa monnieri* treated control rats. Also, the feed and water intake of the epileptic rats were comparatively reduced. *Bacopa monnieri* treatment and carbamazepine treatment reversed these changes to near control level. There was no significant change in the blood glucose in the control and experimental groups of rats. PET imaging studies of glucose metabolism and cerebral blood flow in patients with TLE and depression have so far mainly focused on frontal and temporal lobes, with hippocampus and amygdala being the regions of main interest (Kondziella *et al.*, 2007). The same stress-responsive CNS mediators that produce emotional, cognitive and behavioral manifestations also lead to inhibition of endocrine programs for growth and reproduction to preserve energy, a catabolic state to provide glucose to the brain and increased heart rate and blood pressure (Gold, 2005)

The serotonergic innervation of the cerebral cortex in the rat has been studied by immunohistochemistry employing an antibody directed against the neurotransmitter, serotonin. All regions of the cerebral cortex appear to be innervated by serotonergic axons which have a distinctive morphology: they are fine (0.1–0.5 µm), varicose and extremely convoluted. Serotonergic axons of passage are thicker and comparatively straight.

The serotonergic afferents to the cortex appear to have at least two different modes of distribution, a relatively uniform pattern in the anterior cingulate and the lateral neocortex and a restricted, laminar pattern in the posterior cingulate and the hippocampus. The density and extent of the serotonin innervation is such that the raphe neurons may contact every cell in the cortex. The widespread arborization of serotonin axons contrasts with the spatially restricted termination of thalamic afferents. The distribution of serotonin-containing fibers also differs substantially from the terminal patterns of noradrenergic and dopaminergic fibers. The differences in axonal morphology and distribution amongst the monoamine afferents reflect differences in their contributions to cortical circuitry. The present findings indicate that the serotonin-containing neurons may exert a profound and global, but not necessarily uniform, influence upon cortical function (Lidov, 1980).

Serotonin content

We observed a decrease in the 5-HT content in the cerebral cortex hippocampus, cerebellum and brainstem of epileptic rats when compared to control and *Bacopa monnieri* treated control rats. The monoamine content in brain structures has been related to neuronal excitability and several approaches have been used to study this phenomenon during seizure vulnerability. An increase in the serotonin content was found in cerebral cortex hippocampus, cerebellum and brainstem of *Bacopa monnieri* treated epileptic rats and carbamazepine treated epileptic rats. 5-HT plays an important regulatory role in epileptic mechanism; as demonstrated from studies in both animal models of epilepsy and humans. Reciprocal interactions between the motor system and the serotonergic modulatory system are well documented (Jacobs & Fornal, 1997). In the genetically epilepsy-prone rat model of generalized epilepsy, a decrease is found in brain concentration of serotonin (Dailey *et al.*, 1989). There has been increasing evidence that serotonergic neurotransmission modulates a wide variety of experimentally induced seizures. Generally, agents that elevate extracellular serotonin levels, such as 5-hydroxytryptophan and 5-HT reuptake blockers, inhibit both focal and generalized seizures. Conversely, depletion of brain 5-HT lowers the threshold to audiogenically, chemically and electrically evoked convulsions (Bagdy *et al.*, 2006). Moreover 5-HT is a key modulatory neurotransmitter and has been implicated in the pathophysiology and treatment of anxiety and mood disorders (Neumeister *et al.*, 2002). Both *Bacopa monnieri* and carbamazepine treatment to epileptic rats increased the 5-HT content in brain regions of epileptic rats. *Bacopa monnieri* plant extract is a nerve tonic used extensively in the traditional Indian medicinal system Ayurveda. *Bacopa monnieri* has been used for centuries as a memory-enhancing, antioxidative, adaptogenic (Jyoti & Sharma, 2004), antiinflammatory, analgesic, antipyretic, sedative, and antiepileptic agent. *Bacopa monnieri* is currently recognized as being possibly effective in the treatment of mental illness and epilepsy (Russo *et al.*, 2003).

Cerebral Cortex

5-HT$_{2C}$ receptors are involved in a diversity of physiological functions such as the control of nociception, motor behaviour, endocrine secretion, thermoregulation, modulation of appetite and the control of exchanges between the central nervous system and the cerebrospinal fluid (Tecott *et al.*, 1995; Fone *et al.*, 1998). The cerebellar cortex, like all other motor structures, receives serotonergic innervations in the form of a plexus of fine varicose fibers. (Dieudonné & Dumoulin, 2000).

Our findings report an increase in 5-HT$_{2C}$ receptor function in the cerebral cortex with no significant change in K$_d$ which is supported by the gene expression studies. Increased 5-HT$_{2C}$ receptor function in cortical regions is implicated in mood disorders and anxiodepressive states (Millan, 2005). It has been reported that increased 5-HT$_{2C}$ receptor contributes to the enhanced response to anxiety (Fone *et al.*, 1996) in the epileptic rats. 5-HT$_{2C}$ receptor agonist 1-(m-chlorophenyl) piperazine has been reported to produce hypolocomtion, hypophagia, and anxiogenesis (Samad *et al.*, 2008) in rats. The changes in the receptors have been confirmed using immunofluorescent antibodies specific to 5-HT$_{2C}$ receptors Behavioural and neurochemical evidence for anxiogenic actions of 5-HT$_{2C}$ agonists have been well documented in rodents (Hackler *et al.*, 2007).

The serotonin 5-HT$_{2C}$ receptor subtype signals activate phospholipase C (PLC), leading to the intracellular accumulation of inositol trisphosphate and subsequent Ca^{2+} release. Increased Ca^{2+} release triggers the oxidative damage and excitotoxicity (Bishnoi *et al.*, 2008). Thus up-regulated 5-HT$_{2C}$ receptor function in epileptic cortex leads to excessive Ca^{2+} overload in cells leading to apoptosis. Earlier findings from our lab also implicate overactivation of 5-HT$_{2C}$ receptors in cell proliferation by acting as a co-mitogen (Sudha & Paulose, 1998). Hence, the up-regulated 5-HT$_{2C}$ receptors could play a significant role in neuronal hypertrophy

(Julius *et al.*, 1989) which has been previously reported in cortical regions of patients with temporal lobe epilepsy (Bothwell *et al.*, 2001). At present it is unknown why cortical tissues become epileptogenic. It has been previously demonstrated that in the lateral temporal lobe of TLE patients which are supposed to be normal (Babb *et al.*, 1984) there is fine disorganization in the synaptic circuits that consists of increase and decrease in excitatory and inhibitory synapses respectively (Marco *et al.*, 1997). Neuronal hypertrophy leads to formation of tumours which are reported to be potential causes for onset of secondary seizures (Loscher, 2002). Focal cortical dysplasia is associated with vulnerability to epilepsy, and suggested to augment hippocampal epileptogenicity (Takase *et al.*, 2008) However, its epileptogenicity remains unclear. Therefore, we created a novel rat Serotonin can inhibit events triggered by glutamate release by acting at postsynaptic receptors of the 5-HT_{2C} subtype. Experiments in human cerebral cortex support the view that serotonergic activation through 5-HT_{2C} receptors interacts with glutamate transmission through NMDA receptor (Maura *et al.*, 2000).

Our investigation revealed a down regulation in the NMDA receptor binding in the cerebral cortex of the epileptic rats compared to control and *Bacopa monnieri* treated without a change in its affinity. Also, there was increase in the gene expression of 5-HT_{2C} and mGlu5 gene expression whereas a decrease in the expression NMDA2b of in the cerebral cortex of epileptic. *Bacopa monnieri* and carbamazepine treatment to epileptic rats showed a reversal of the receptor expressions to near control. These have been confirmed using immunofluorescent antibodies specific to $5\text{-HT}_{2C,}$ NMDA2b and mGlu5 receptors in our study. Conflicting reports exist regarding the status of NMDA receptors in the epileptic cortex. Guzman *et al.*, (2008) reported neuronal network hyperexcitability due to NMDA receptors in the deep layers of entorhinal cortex of pilocarpine treated rats. But we report a decrease in the NMDA receptor activity in the epileptic cortex. A possible explanation to the loss of NMDA binding sites is suggested to be due to a compensatory down-regulation of the receptors because of an excessive release of glutamate (Otoya *et al.*, 1997) during epilepsy. Hypofunction of NMDA receptor has been indicated to produce schizophrenic symptoms, including deficits in working memory (Olney and Farber, 1995). NMDA-receptor antagonism could adversely affect storage and processing of information (Javitt *et al.*, 1996) in the cerebral cortex of epileptic rats. Our recent studies involving Water Maze Test (Reas *et al.*, 2008) confirms the deficits in memory and cognitive impairments observed in the epileptic rats.

Immunohistochemical studies have previously identified positive staining for presynaptic mGlu5 receptors in the rat cerebral cortex (Romano *et al.*, 1995). The mGluR5 is reported to mediate a G-protein-dependent release of intracellular calcium stores (Valenti *et al.*, 2002). Moreover, NMDA receptor function is inhibited by a rise in intracellular calcium (Rosenmund *et al.*, 1995). Yu *et al.*, (1997) pointed out that mGlu5 mediated direct inhibition *via* G-proteins also leads to NMDA receptor inhibition. We observed an increased expression of the mGluR5 receptor gene expression in the cerebral cortex of epileptic rats compared to control and *Bacopa monneiri* treated control rats. Hence, it is likely that the G-protein-dependent release of intracellular Ca^{2+} through mGlu5 activation depresses NMDA responses as seen in our present study.

Our experimental findings also demonstrate an increase in intracellular IP3 content in the epileptic cerebral cortex. Inositol phosphates are known to regulate membrane trafficking, glucose metabolism, cytoskeletal organisation and intracellular Ca^{2+} homeostasis—particularly the release of stored Ca^{2+} *via* IP3 receptors. Intracellular Ca^{2+} regulation by both inositol 1,4,5-triphosphate receptors (IP3R) and ryanodine receptors (RyR) has been implicated in epileptogenesis and the maintenance of epilepsy (Nagarkatti *et al.*, 2008). This leads to excess Ca^{2+} release from IP3-sensitive stores in response both $5\text{-}HT_{2C}$ receptor hyperfunction and mGluR5 stimulation. Excessive Ca^{2+} overload in cells have been reported to cause apoptosis. Boehning *et al.*, (2003) demonstrated a small amount of cytochrome C released from mitochondria binds to and promote Ca^{2+} conductance through IP3 in the endoplamic reticulum membrane. The released Ca^{2+} further triggers mass exodus of cytochrome C from all mitochodria in the cell and thus activating the caspase and nuclease enzyme that finalize the apoptotic process. Glutamate uptake into neurons and glial cells is important for the termination of glutamatergic transmission. They are essential for the maintenance of low extracellular levels of glutamate (Lo'pez-Bayghen *et al.*, 2003). We observed an increase in the expression of GLAST receptor gene expression of epileptic rats. The increase in the glutamate transporter is suggested to be a compensatory mechanism to facilitate the fast removal of the glutamate and thus prevents its prolonged action at the synapse during the epileptic condition.

Treatment with *Bacopa monnieri* to epileptic rats caused a reversal in the B_{max} of $5\text{-}HT_{2C}$ receptors and NMDA receptors to near control level. It is also evident that *Bacopa monnieri* has neuroprotective action mediated through the $5\text{-}HT_{2C}$, NMDA2b, mGlu5 and GLAST receptor at the transcription level. Singh *et al.*, 2006 have demonstrated the anti-oxidant properties of *Bacopa monnieri* in rodents. *Bacopa monnieri* treatment has been demonstrated to modulate serotonin level (Singh *et al.*, 1997) which renders protection against seizures (Reas *et al.*, 2008) during epilepsy. However, its traditional memory-enhancing claim could be established experimentally by our findings on $5\text{-}HT_{2C}$ and NMDA receptors. *Bacopa monniera* treatment to epileptic rats significantly increases NMDA receptors which play an important role in cognition and memory. Also, *Bacopa monnieri* treatment has been reported to possess anxiolytic and antidepressant property which is evident from modulation of 5-HT$_{2C}$ receptors. Up regulation of the 5-HT$_{2C}$ receptor renders the epileptic rat anxiogenic which is supported by elevated plus maze test. *Bacopa monnieri* treatment to epileptic rats caused the upregulated 5-HT$_{2C}$ receptors and IP3 content to near control level and thus provides support at the molecular level to the antidepressive and anxiolytic property as provided by reports of Bhattacharya & Ghosal, (1998) and Sairam *et al.,* (2002).

To determine anxiety in experimental groups, rats were subjected to the elevated plus maze. Behaviour in rodents is determined by the conflict between the drive to explore the unknown area/object and the motivation to avoid potential danger. Elevated open alleys arouse greater avoidance responses than elevated closed alleys. Voluntary passage onto the open arms of an elevated, plus shaped maze is associated with neurobiological changes indicative of a decreased anxiety (Olivier *et al.,* 2008). In elevated plus maze test, the epileptic rats exhibit significant alterations in its behavioural response due to epileptic insult to the cortical neurons. The epileptic rats remained for longer period in closed arms of elevated plus-maze which is characteristic to anxio-depressive traits. It has been demonstrated that the preference shown for the closed arms reflects an aversion toward the open arms, caused by fear or anxiety induced by the open space in the elevated plus maze test (de Souza *et al.,* 2007). The head dipping attempt, stretched attend posture and grooming attempts were also greatly reduced supporting the anxiogenic condition as a result of epileptic stress. But an increased attempt made towards open arm entry by epileptic rats indicates an abnormal behavioural profile. 5-HT$_{2C}$ selective antagonists show robust anxiolytic-like effects in conflict-based paradigms, so the activity of S32006 in the Vogel's Confidence Test can confidently be ascribed to 5-HT$_{2C}$ receptor blockade (Martin *et al.* 2002; Millan 2003). The *Bacopa monnieri* treatment during epilepsy reversed the behavioural abnormalities to control. *Bacopa monnieri* treatment to epileptic rats had anti-anxiety effects, as indicated by increase of the time spent in the open arm and increase in head dipping attempt, stretched attend posture and grooming attempts compared to epileptic rats.

Thus we show evidence for dysfunction of the epileptic cerebral cortex that is a reflection for manifestation of abnormal behavioural patterns and possibility for cellular proliferation. The receptor analysis and gene expression studies along with the behavioural data implicate a role for $5\text{-}HT_{2C}$ receptors in the manifestation of anxiety and NMDA receptors for the cognitive and memory deficits associated with epileptic rats. It is evident that neuroprotective role of *Bacopa monnieri* in epilepsy involves the interaction of $5\text{-}HT_{2C}$ and NMDA receptors, with modulation of mGlu5 and GLAST receptor gene expression at the mRNA level and IP3 and cGMP activation at the second messenger level. Thus our results suggest that anti-epileptic effect of *Bacopa monnieri* extract is mediated through $5\text{-}HT_{2C}$, NMDA receptors, mGlu5, GLAST, IP3 and cGMP functional regulation which has clinical significance in the treatment of epilepsy.

Hippocampus

Hippocampus is an area of interest to investigate the pilocarpine-induced seizures, because it is one of the most vulnerable brain areas for epilepsy-related brain damage and plays a main role in the development and maintenance of limbic seizures. A wide range of neuropsychological deficits follow the SE, which typically include learning and memory dysfunction and other cognitive deficits (Holmes *et al.*, 2004; Holmes, 2006). The hippocampal formation contains a rich glutamatergic and GABA-ergic input, GABA-ergic interneurones containing peptide co-transmitters and the glutamatergic perforant pathway interconnects with entorhinal cortex, subiculum,

CA1, CA3 fields and dentate gyrus (Ottersen & Storm-Mathisen, 1984). Pilocarpine produced marked changes in morphology, membrane properties and synaptic responses of hippocampal rat neurons which are comparable to those observed in human epileptic hippocampal neurones (Isokawa & Mello, 1991). Recent findings suggest that the SE induced by pilocarpine is triggered by changes in the blood-brain barrier permeability.

We observed a decrease in the serotonin content in the hippocampus of epileptic rats when compared to control and *Bacopa monnieri* treated control rats. Studies of the serotonergic modulation of hippocampal function have been complicated by the marked heterogeneity of 5-HT receptor subtypes, with at least 14 distinct subtypes expressed in the central nervous system. Psychological stress activates the serotonergic neurons in the hippocampus and the amygdala through the cortical association areas and through ascending catecholaminergic neurons from the brain stem (Feldman & Weidenfeld 1998; Koob & Heinrichs 1999). Serotonergic neurotransmission exerts a considerable influence on hippocampal function. This structure is influenced powerfully by serotonergic projections from midbrain raphe nuclei (Tecott *et al.*, 1998) which modulate hippocampal electrical activity, hippocampal-dependent behaviours, and long-term potentiation (LTP), a form of hippocampal plasticity that has been implicated in memory formation (Vanderwolf & Baker, 1986). There is good evidence that noradrenaline and 5-HT interact to influence neuroplasticity in the brain (Delgado 2004). Many modern antidepressants including mirtazapine, milnacipran, venlafaxine, and duloxetine have been developed based on their interaction with both 5-HT and noradrenaline (Tran *et al.* 2003).

In this study, we focused on the 5-HT_{2C} receptor, which is abundantly expressed throughout the hippocampal formation and the subiculum. An involvement of this receptor subtype is suggested in the regulation of neuronal plasticity (Tecott,

1998). We observed a significant increase in the B_{max} and K_d of 5-HT$_{2C}$ receptors the hippocampus of epileptic rats compared to control and *Bacopa monnieri*. 5-HT$_{2C}$ receptors gene expression patterns were similar to the receptor binding studies. Treatment with *Bacopa monnieri* and carbamazepine reversed the receptor alterations in Bmax and K_d to near control levels. Anxiolytic like actions of 5-HT$_{2C}$ receptor antagonists, transduced in the amygdala and hippocampus (Menard & Treit 1999; Campbell & Merchant 2003; Millan 2003; Alves *et al.* 2004), may be expressed against certain forms of clinical anxiety. 5-HT$_{2C}$ receptor antagonism have been reported to improve insomnia and sexual dysfunction comorbid to depression (Dekeyne *et al.*, 2008). *Bacopa monnieri*'s multiple active constituents have multifunctional properties, making its pharmacology complex. *Bacopa monnieri* treatment has been demonstrated to increase serotonin levels in hippocampus (Singh & Dhawan, 1997) preventing the compensatory increase in the number of 5-HT$_{2C}$ receptor in the epileptic hippocampus and thus provide protection to hippocampus during seizures.

Based on extensive supportive experimental data, the release of high levels of glutamate by neurons at a seizure focus is thought to be the underlying mechanism for the initiation and maintenance of seizures. Imbalances between excitatory and inhibitory synaptic transmission in key brain areas such as hippocampus are implicated in the pathophysiology of TLE, in which fast synaptic excitatory neurotransmission is mediated *via* activation of ionotropic glutamate receptors like NMDA receptors.

We report a down regulation in the NMDA receptor binding in the hippocampus of the epileptic rats compared to control with an increase in its affinity. The gene expression of NMDA2b sub unit was also found to be decreased in the epileptic hippocampus. *Bacopa monnieri* treatment and carbamazepine treatment caused an increase in the NMDA receptors and NMDA2b gene expression to near control level. There was no significant change in K_d of epileptic rats treated with carbamazepine compared to epileptic rats. The mGlu5 and GLAST gene expression was also found to be increased in the epileptic hippocampus. *Bacopa monnieri* treatment and carbamazepine treatment reversed these changes in the gene expression to near control level. Our experimental results also show an increase in the IP3, cGMP and cAMP content in the hippocampus of epileptic rats compared to control and *Bacopa monnieri* treated control rats. *Bacopa monnieri* and carbamazepine treatment to epileptic rats showed a reversal in the alterations to control level.

A possible explanation to the loss of NMDA binding sites in the epileptic hippocampus is suggested to be due to a compensatory down-regulation of the receptors because of an excessive release of glutamate in the epileptic hippocampus (Otoya *et al.*, 1997, Reas *et al.*, 2008) or loss of cells in the sclerotic hippocampus (Steffens *et al.*, 2005) during epilepsy. Hippocampal area CA3 is critically involved in the formation of nonoverlapping neuronal subpopulations to store memory representations as distinct events. Efficient pattern separation relies on the strong and sparse excitatory input from the mossy fibers to pyramidal cells and feed forward inhibitory interneurons (Galván *et al.*, 2008). Several studies have shown an increase in the density of hippocampal and cortical NMDA receptors in some animal models of epilepsy (Yeh *et al.*, 1989; Ekonomou & Angelatou, 1999). Other experiments in epileptic human and rat neocortex, showed that components of the NMDA-receptor complex were downregulated (Wyneken *et al.*, 2003). Our experimental results support the latter. Earlier studies described that intrahippocampal administration of pilocarpine resulted in a decrease of the extracellular glutamate and shows simultaneous slowing of the rhythmic activity recorded on the electroencephalogram (EEG), showing theta and delta waves. Intrahippocampal pilocarpine perfusion followed by a significant and sustained enhancement of the extracellular glutamate concentrations was reported. (Smolders *et al.*, 2004). Reports also suggest that seizures induced either by tetanus toxin or flurothyl were found to reduce the expression of NMDA receptor subunits in both the hippocampus and neocortex (Hashimoto *et al.*, 2004). Enhanced glutamate in the EC is suggested to be associated with the development of epileptic condition (Thompson *et al.*, 2007). Recent research suggests that the consolidation of fear and extinction memories depends on NMDA receptors. Using a fear conditioning and extinction paradigm in healthy normal volunteers, it was shown that post-learning administration of the NMDA partial agonist D-cycloserine facilitates fear memory consolidation (Kalisch *et al.*, 2009).

Our experimental results showed that *Bacopa monnieri* treatment caused an increase in total NMDA receptors and K_d as well as gene expression of NMDA2b to near control level. We had previously reported a down regulated NMDAR1 gene expression during epilepsy which was reversed to control level after *Bacopa monnieri* treatment (Reas *et al.*, 2008). NMDA receptor in the hippocampus is reported to modulate some forms of memory formation, with the NR2b subunit being particularly relevant to this process (White & Youngentoba, 2004). It is evident that *Bacopa monnieri* has a definite role in decreasing glutamate mediated excitotoxicity in the hippocampus of epileptic rats. Treatment with *Bacopa monnieri* extract reduced the increase in glutamate dehydrogenase activity to near-control levels and was effective in memory enhancement in epileptic rats which was observed through the Water Maze Test (Reas *et al.*, 2008; Paulose *et al.*, 2008) This is consistent with earlier reports (Singh *et al.*, 1988) that *Bacopa monnieri* treatment can induce membrane dephosphorylation and a concomitant increase in mRNA turnover and protein synthesis. It can also enhance protein kinase activity in the hippocampus, which is critically involved in learning and memory.

The mGluR5 is reported to mediate a G-protein-dependent release of intracellular calcium stores (Valenti *et al.*, 2002). Moreover, NMDA receptor function is inhibited by a rise in intracellular calcium (Rosenmund *et al.*, 1995). Yu *et al.*, (1997) pointed out that mGlu5 mediated direct inhibition *via* G-proteins also leads to NMDA receptor inhibition. mGluR5 receptors may modulate NMDA receptor function because both receptors have been linked as signaling partners (Kotecha *et al.* 2003; Movsesyan *et al.* 2001). We observed an increased expression of the mGluR5 receptor in the cerebral cortex of epileptic rats compared to control and *Bacopa monneiri* treated control rats. Hence, it is likely that the G-protein-dependent release of intracellular Ca^{2+} through mGlu5 activation depresses NMDA responses as seen in our present study. MGluR5 antagonists are promising candidates for anti-depressants (Stachowicz *et al.* 2006).

Our experiment with the second messengers revealed an increased level of IP3, cGMP and cAMP in the hippocampus of epileptic rats compared to control and *Bacopa monnieri* treated control rats. Both *Bacopa monnieri* and carbamazepine treatment to epileptic rats reversed these changes to control values. Mossy fiber sprouting, gliosis, and synaptic reorganization in the hippocampus, amygdala, parahippocampal cortices and thalamus during temporal lobe seizures participates in the constitution of hyperexcitable circuits underlying spontaneous seizures and emotional disturbances (Roch *et al.* 2002). Antiepileptic agents reduce aggression in rats (Keele 2001) and humans (Stanford *et al.* 2005).

Cerebellum

In our earlier studies, we reported the therapeutic action of *Bacopa monnieri* on glutamate receptors especially in the cerebellum and hippocampus of pilocarpine induced epilepsy in rats (Reas *et al.*, 2008, Paulose *et al.*, 2008). In the present study, we have demonstrated the therapeutic role of *Bacopa monnieri* in epileptic motor dysfunction through its effect on $5\text{-}HT_{2C}$ receptor gene expression and binding in cerebellum. Electrophysiologists have reported that serotonergic agonists affect directly the firing of cerebellar neurons (Cumming-Hood *et al.*, 1993) and are able to modulate the effect of excitatory amino acids. Experimental evidence indicate the involvement of the cerebellum in variety of human mental activities including language, attention, cognitive affective syndromes (Gowen and Miall, 2005) fear and anxiety caused by threats of pain (Ploghause *et al.*, 1999) and motor relearning (Imazumi *et al.*, 2004). There is also accumulating evidence to suggest that the cerebellum plays a role in more cognitive, social and emotional functions (Allen *et al.*, 1997; Schmahmann and Sherman, 1998). some of the most frequent signs of cerebellar hypoplasia include poor fine motor skills, hypotonia and autistic features (Wassmer *et al.*, 2003). The cerebellar vermis integrates and processes the inputs from the vestibular, visual and proprioceptive systems to coordinate muscle timing as a result of which the centre of gravity stays within the limits of stable upright standing (Diener *et al.*, 1989). Damage to the cerebellum, in particular the vermis (Baloh *et al.*, 1998) results in more postural sway than in control subjects (Ho *et al.*, 2004, Marvel *et al.*, 2004). Decreased postural stability would correspond with abnormalities of the vermis observed in autistic subjects (Gowen & Miall, 2005).

$5\text{-}HT_{2C}$ receptors exist in the rat cerebellum and they participate in the processing and integration of sensory information, regulation of the monoaminergic system modulation of neuroendocrine regulation, anxiety and feeding behaviour (Tecott *et al.*, 1995). Our investigation revealed a decrease in the 5-HT content and $5\text{-}HT_{2C}$ receptor binding in the cerebellum of the epileptic rats compared to control with an increased affinity. Decreased serotonin in the brain has previously been implicated in development and spread of seizures (Dailey *et al.*, 1989). This decreased

5-HT$_{2C}$ receptor binding in the cerebellum is suggested to contribute towards a lowered threshold and a rapid progression of seizure activity in the epileptic rats. Previously, mesulergine (2 or 4 mg/kg), administered prior to electroshock testing, have shown to recapitulate epileptic syndrome associated with sporadic spontaneous seizures in the 5-HT$_{2C}$ mutant phenotype in wild-type mice (Applegate & Tecott, 1998).

Treatment with *Bacopa monnieri* to epileptic rats caused a reversal in the B$_{max}$ of 5-HT$_{2C}$ receptors to near control level. Rohini *et al.*, (2004) have demonstrated the anti-oxidant properties of *Bacopa monnieri* in rodents. This is in consistence with the earlier reports (Reas *et al.*, 2008) which states that *Bacopa monnieri* treatment induces membrane dephosphorylation and concomitant increase in mRNA turnover and protein synthesis. Moreover, *Bacopa monnieri* treatment has been demonstrated to increase serotonin level (Singh & Dhawan, 1997) which renders protection against seizures (Bagdy, 2006) during epilepsy.

We also observed an increase in the NMDA receptors binding, NMDA2b and mGlu5 gene expression in the cerebellum of epileptic rats compared to control rats and *Bacopa monnieri* treated control rats. In the cerebellum of pilocarpine induced epileptic rats, extracellular glutamate was reported to be elevated significantly during the pilocarpine-induced convulsions. During limbic seizures and during the interictal period, changes in metabolic activity and cerebral blood flow occur (Park *et al.*, 1992). Hyperperfusion at the ipsilateral side of epileptic focus, as demonstrated in a case report (Overbeck *et al.*, 1990) explain the increased amino acid and thus glutamate concentrations in ipsilateral cerebellum.

Pharmacological tools now allow for the examination of the role of metabotropic glutamate receptors (mGluRs) in the development of sensitization (Spooren *et al.* 2000). mGluRs regulate synaptic transmission by modulating calcium and potassium channels and the activity of ionotropic glutamate receptors. mGluR5 receptors modulate NMDA receptor function because both receptors have been linked as signaling partners (O'Leary *et al.* 2000; Movsesyan *et al.* 2001; Kotecha *et al.* 2003). The activation of mGluR5 receptors leads to the potentiation of NMDA currents (Bleakman *et al.* 1992; Cerne and Randic 1992), possibly through the activation of protein kinase C and the subsequent increase in intracellular Ca^{2+}, thereby acting as an indirect agonist of NMDA receptors (Benquet *et al.* 2002; Fujii *et al.* 2004). NMDA receptor activation in the cerebellum leads to an increase in the Ca^{2+} also *via* IP3 receptors. Glutamate uptake into neurons and glia cells is important for the termination of glutamatergic transmission. Several glutamate transporters have been characterized, the Na^{+}-dependent glutamate/aspartate transporter (GLAST) being the major uptake system within the cerebellum. We observed a down regulation in the GLAST expression in the cerebellum of epileptic rats. *Bacopa monnieri* treatment and carbamazepine treatment reversed the changes to near control. The decreased expression of the GLAST gene expression causes a low uptake of glutamate in the cerebellum. Purkinje cells make synaptic contacts with the parallel fibers, which are the axons of the granule cells and that these synapses are glutamatergic, it is possible that glutamate synaptic levels regulate the Bergmann glia glutamate transporter, GLAST. In fact, it has been suggested that glutamate regulates GLAST translocation process in these cells in a receptor-independent manner (Gonzalez & Ortega, 2000). Thus, *Bacopa monnieri* treatment renders protection by increasing the glutamate re-uptake into cerebellar cells and thus reducing the extracellular glutamate which cause excitotoxicity.

Our experimental results also show an increase in the IP3, cGMP and cAMP content in the cerebellum of epileptic rats compared to control and *Bacopa monnieri* treated control rats. *Bacopa monnieri* and carbamazepine treatment to epileptic rats reversed the increase in the IP3, cGMP and cAMP levels to near control.

The increased cGMP content in the epileptic cerebellum is due to the increased NMDA receptors. Suvarna and O'Donnel, (2002) reported the NMDA mediated increase in the cGMP in the neuronal culture studies. Baltrons *et al.*, (1997) and Oh *et al.*, (1997) reported an NMDA induce cGMP formation in the cultured cerebellar granule cells. Increased IP3 activation leads to Ca^{2+} influx which in turn activates neuronal nitric oxide synthase (nNOS) to produce NO (Garthwaite, 2005). NO activates soluble guanylyl cyclase (sGC) to generate increased levels of cGMP which in turn activates protein kinase G (PKG) (Garthwaite, 2005) in the cerebellum during epilepsy. The role of NO during epileptogenesis is controversial as it has been shown to have both anticonvulsant (Sardo & Ferraro, 2007; Royes *et al.*, 2007)) and proconvulsant (De Sarro *et al.*, 1993; Tutka *et al.*, 1996). This rise in cAMP could be mainly due to the influence of increased mGlu5 (Winder & Conn, 1992) receptors as is seen our studies. Thus the neuroprotective effect of *Bacopa monnieri* involves the modulation at the second messenger level also.

We observed a down regulation of the 5-HT_{2C} receptor expression using immunofluorescent antibodies specific to 5-HT_{2C}. *Bacopa monnieri* and carbamazepine treatment to epileptic rats reversed the alteration to near control, thus confirming the gene expression studies in the cerebellum of epileptic rats. Also, there was increase in the gene expression of NMDA2b and mGlu5 gene expression in the cerebellum of epileptic and these have been confirmed using immunofluorescent antibodies specific to NMDA2b and mGlu5 receptors in our study. *Bacopa monnieri* and carbamazepine treatment to epileptic rats reversed the alteration to near control, thus confirming the gene expression studies in the cerebellum of epileptic rats.

Rotarod test has been previously used to examine motor in-coordination (Cendelín *et al.*, 2008). The rotarod experiment demonstrated the impairment in the motor function and coordination in the epileptic rats. Epileptic rats showed lower fall off time from the rotating rod when compared to control suggesting impairment in their ability to integrate sensory input with appropriate motor commands to balance their posture and at the same time adjust their limb movements on the metallic rod and is indicative of cerebellar dysfunction. Many other brain regions have been associated with timing tasks including the dorsal lateral premotor cortex, inferior parietal lobe, supplementary motor area, superior temporal gyrus, caudal putamen, ventrolateral thalamus and inferior frontal gyrus (Rao *et al.*, 1997; Jancke *et al.*, 2000; Lewis and Miall, 2003). Abnormalities of some of these areas, such as the inferior frontal gyrus and superior temporal gyrus (Abell *et al.*, 1999; Castelli *et al.*, 2002) have been reported in autistic subjects rendering it difficult to isolate the cerebellum in this task. However, increased timing variance has been observed in patients with cerebellar disorders (Ivry *et al.*, 1988). Loss of coordination of motor movement, inability to judge distance and timing, incapacity to perform rapid alternating movements and hypotonia has been reported during cerebellar damage (Gowen and Miall, 2005). Poor limb - eye coordination in patients with cerebellar dysfunction has been earlier report (Van Donkelaar and Lee, 1994).

Thus perturbations of the 5-HT_{2C} receptor system directly modulate seizure susceptibility. This study demonstrates the involvement of 5-HT_{2C} receptor which has modulating effect on the seizure susceptibility and associated motor defects. The administration of crude extract of *Bacopa monnieri* to epileptic rats increased the fall off time from the rod when compared to control rats. *Bacopa monnieri* not only possesses memory enhancing properties but also alleviate their stress levels which assist in lowering their time for spatial recognition (Shankar & Singh, 2000) and helps to maintain their posture during movement on the rod. It is also reported to facilitate the acquisition, consolidation, retention and recall of learned asks (Diener etal., 1989) and improves the speed at which visual information is processed.

To summarize, our findings suggest dysfunction of the epileptic cerebellum that is a reflection of cerebellar serotonergic and glutamatergic abnormality. The receptor analysis and gene expression studies along with the behavioural data implicate a role for serotonin, 5-HT_{2C}, NMDA and mGlu5 receptors in the modulation of neuronal network excitability and seizure propagation *via* changes in IP3, cGMP and cAMP. These neurofunctional deficits are one of the key contributors to motor deficits and stress associated with epilepsy. Our results suggest that *Bacopa monnieri* extract treatment reverses the 5-HT_{2C} receptor mediated motor dysfunction in epilepsy and cerebellar excitotoxicity due to glutamatergic modulation mediated through changes in IP3, cGMP and cAMP. This will have clinical significance in the management of epilepsy.

Brain stem

We found a decrease in the serotonin content in the brainstem of epileptic rats when compared to control and *Bacopa monnieri* treated control rats. The cell bodies of the 5-HT containing neurons are confined primarily to the raphe nucleus of the brainstem (Duan *et al.*, 1989; Jocobs and Azimitia, 1992) where the level of extracellular 5-HT are determined (Sharp *et al.*, 1990). 5-HT plays an important regulatory role in epileptic mechanisms; as demonstrated from studies in both animal models of epilepsy and humans. Selective serotonin reuptake inhibitors (SSRIs) such as fluoxetine, which has antiseizure effects in several models (Hernandez *et al.*, 2002). In the genetically epilepsy-prone rat model of generalized epilepsy, a decrease is found in brain concentration of serotonin (Dailey *et al.*, 1989). Serotonin is reported to play a role in the mechanism of action of some antiepileptic drugs (AEDs). Studies in genetically epilepsy prone rats GEPRs suggest that carbamazepine (CBZ) and valproate (VPA) release 5-HT. (Yan, 2002, Yan *et al.*, 1992, Dailey *et al.*, 1997). Decrease in the serotonin content is thus involved the seizure generation in epileptic rats. After *Bacopa monnieri and* carbamazepine treatment, an increase in the serotonin content towards control level was found. Thus, *Bacopa monnieri* treatment to epileptic rats causes an increase in the serotonin content in the brainstem.

Our experimental results showed a decrease in the B_{max} and K_d and gene expression pattern of 5-HT$_{2C}$ receptors in the brainstem of epileptic rats compared to control and *Bacopa monnieri* treated control rats. *Bacopa monnieri* and carbamazepine treatment reserved these receptor changes to control level.

There was an increase in the B_{max} of NMDA receptors with a decreased K_d when compared to control and *Bacopa monnieri* treated control rats. The NMDA2b mGlu5 and GLAST gene expression was found to be up- regulated in the brainstem of epileptic rats when compared to control and *Bacopa monnieri* treated control rats. Our results showed that there is an increased glutamatergic activity in the brain stem during chronic epileptic state. Increased NMDA receptors in the brain regions are involved in repetitive tonic seizures during epilepsy. In the epileptic rats group treated with *Bacopa monnieri* and carbamazepine the B_{max} reversed to the control. NMDA2b and mGlu 5 and GLAST gene expression gene expression also reversed to the control values. These results suggest the therapeutic effect of *Bacopa monnieri* in epilepsy through NMDA and mGlu5 receptors. It is widely accepted that excitatory amino-acid neutransmitters such as glutamate are involved in the initiation of seizures and their propagation. Most attention is directed to synapses using NMDA receptors but more recent evidence indicates potential roles for ionotropic non-NMDA (AMPA/kainate) and metabotropic glutamate receptors (Ure *et al.*, 2006).

Based on the role of glutamate in the development and expression of seizures, antagonism of glutamate receptors has long been thought to provide a rational strategy in the search for new, effective anticonvulsant drugs. Furthermore, glutamate receptor antagonists, particularly those acting on NMDA receptors, protect effectively in the induction of kindling. It was suggested that they have utility in epilepsy prophylaxis. However, many clinical trials with competitive and uncompetitive NMDA receptor antagonists in patients with partial seizures showed that these drugs lack convincing anticonvulsant activity but induce severe neurotoxic adverse effects in doses which were well tolerated in healthy volunteers. The proconvulsant effects of NMDA were reported when administered 30 minutes before pilocarpine injection. Smaller and higher doses of NMDA drugs not protected but increased pilocarpine-induced seizures and mortality. (Frietas *et al.*, 2006). NMDA antagonists, irrespective whether they are competitive, high- or lowaffinity uncompetitive, glycine site or polyamine site antagonists, do not counteract focal seizure activity. They attenuate propagation to secondarily generalized seizures indicating that once kindling is established, NMDA receptors are not critical for the expression of fully kindled seizures (Locher & Honak, 1991) in brainstem.

Taken together, the reports suggest that recurrent seizures produce persistent decreases in molecular markers for glutamatergic synapses - particularly components of the NMDA receptor complex implicated in learning and memory. Mitsuyoshi *et al.*, (1993) reported that NMDA receptors were down regulated due to repetitive tonic seizures in double mutant spontaneously epileptic rats. The possible role of altered genetic expression in mediating symptomatic epilepsy represents a molecular mechanism that could account for long-lasting changes in neuronal function in response to environmental influences (DeLorenzo, 1991). If changes in genetic expression underlie epilepsy, long lasting alterations in transcriptional regulation should accompany epileptogenesis. Previous reports indicate that epilepsy induced by SE in the pilocarpine model is associated with a long lasting increase in the binding of the transcription factor SRF to its DNA consensus sequence.

We observed an increase in the IP3 and cGMP levels while a decrease in the cAMP level in the brainstem of epileptic rats compared to control and *Bacopa monnieri* treated control rats. NMDA receptor activation has been implicated in IP3 mediated and cGMP signalling pathway by Suvarna and O'Donnel, (2002). Winder and Conn (1993) reported the involvement of mGlu5 receptors on cAMP activation. But in our study, the cAMP levels are low inspite of increased mGlu5 gene expression indicating the involvement of other receptors on the functional modulation of cAMP in the epileptic brainstem.

Feelings of despair, depressive mood, aggressive behaviour, anxiety, memory impairment and overt psychosis are among the common psychiatric features in patients with TLE (Kanner 2006; Blumer *et al.* 2004). Monoaminergic neurotransmitters such as 5-HT and noradrenaline interact with glutamatergic metabolite, which leads to disturbances of neuronal circuits. Atrophy of hippocampus and memory impairment develops, as do transient hypertrophy of amygdala and impaired fear processing. As the hippocampus has critical implications for both seizure activity and mood disorders, this area provides a link between epilepsy and depression (Hajszan & MacLusky 2006). The structural and functional alterations from one disease evoke the other and *vice versa*. In TLE, for instance, hyperexcitability and neuronal cell loss in the limbic system evokes mood disturbances, whereas hippocampal atrophy and neurotransmitter disturbances in depression decreases the seizure threshold and ultimately lead to TLE. Hence, the social interaction test and forced swim test which are commonly used paradigms for models of anxiodepressive states, was conducted.

In the social interaction test, epileptic rats spent less time in active interactions in the novel environment. Attempts at allogrooming, sniffing the partner, following were reduced when compared to control rats and *Bacopa monnieri* treated control rats. Administration of *Bacopa monnieri* treatment to epileptic rats resulted in an increase in the time spent in social interaction to near control values. Patients with intractable TLE exhibit an increased risk of psychiatric comorbidity, including depression, anxiety, psychosis, and learning disorders (Gastens *et al.*, 2008). 5-HT_{2C} receptor agonists likewise decrease social interaction. Though an inhibitory influence upon motor function suggests caution in the interpretation of these data, their influence on cellular markers and clinical studies also suggest anxiogenic-like effects (Hackler *et al.* 2007). 5-HT_{2C} antagonists consistently enhance active social interaction in rats.

The forced swim test, the space for rat's movement was restricted from which they cannot escape. The period of immobility was greater in epileptic rats compared to control and *Bacopa monnieri* treated control rats. *Bacopa monnieri* treatment once daily over a period of 15 days decreased the period of immobility in the epileptic rats. Carbamzepine treatment to epileptic rats also showed a similar effect. Immobility in rats is considered to be a state of lowed mood or hopelessness which the rodent experience when they are forced to swim in a constrained space from they cannot escape. This is believed to indicate a failure or reduced attempts towards escape directed behaviour from persistent stress. It also causes the development of passive behaviour that disengages the animal from coping up with stressful stimuli. This form of immobility which is a state of despair is reported to be reduced by a broad spectrum of anti-depressant drugs (Porsolt *et al.*, 1977).

Our experimental results thus support the anticonvulsant property of *Bacopa monnieri* at the molecular level. We conclude from our studies that *Bacopa monnieri* extract treatment potentates a therapeutic effect by reversing the alterations in 5-HT$_{2C}$ and NMDA receptor binding, gene expression for NMDA2b, mGlu5 receptor and GLAST along with IP3, cGMP and cAMP that occur during epilepsy, resulting in reduced glutamate-mediated excitotoxity in the overstimulated brain regions. Thus, it is evident that *Bacopa monnieri* treatment to epileptic rats renders protection against seizure related excitotoxicity, associated with motor and cognitive deficits which will have therapeutic significance in the management of epilepsy.

Summary

1) Pilocarpine induced TLE rats were used as a model to study the alterations of serotoninergic, ionotropic and metabotropic receptors and their functional regulation by *Bacopa monnieri*. It was used to study the serotonin, 5-HT$_{2C}$ and NMDA receptor alterations in the epileptic rats, *Bacopa monnieri* and carbamazepine treatment to epileptic rats.

2) The body weight, feed and water intake was carried out to analyze the changes in body weight, feed and water consumption due to seizures in epileptic rats compared to control and effect of *Bacopa monnieri* and carbamazepine treatment to epileptic rats. Epilepsy caused a reduction in the body weight, food and water consumption. *Bacopa monnieri* and carbamazepine treatment to epileptic rats reversed the changes to near control.

3) Blood glucose level in the serum was measured to analyze the circulating glucose level changes due to seizures in epileptic rats compared to control and the effect of *Bacopa monnieri* and carbamazepine treatment to epileptic rats. Epilepsy did not cause any significant change in the circulating blood glucose level of epileptic rats. There was no significant change in the circulating blood glucose of epileptic rats after treatment with *Bacopa monnieri* and carbamazepine.

4) The 5-HT and 5-HIAA contents were measured to identify its alteration in the cerebral cortex, hippocampus, cerebellum and brainstem in epileptic rats compared to control and effect of *Bacopa monnieri* and carbamazepine treatment to epileptic rats using High Performance Liquid Chromatography.

a.   Significant decrease in 5-HT content in the cerebral cortex, hippocampus, cerebellum and brainstem was observed in epileptic rats compared to control rats and *Bacopa monnieri* treated control rats. *Bacopa monnieri* and carbamazepine treatment to epileptic rats reversed the 5-HT content to control level.

b.   5-HIAA content significantly increased the cerebral cortex, hippocampus, cerebellum and brainstem of epileptic rats compared to control rats and *Bacopa monnieri* treated control rats. *Bacopa monnnieri* treatment to epileptic rats reversed the changes to near control level.

c.   5-HT/5-HIAA ratio decreased significantly in the cerebral cortex, hippocampus, cerebellum and brainstem of epileptic compared to control rats and *Bacopa monnieri* treated control rats. *Bacopa monnieri* treatment to epileptic rats reversed the changes to control in cerebral cortex and cerebellum.

5) $5\text{-}HT_{2C}$ receptor functional status was analysed by Scatchard analysis using $[^{3}H]$mesulergine in cerebral cortex, hippocampus, brainstem and cerebellum. Receptor gene expression was confirmed by Real-Time PCR. The $5\text{-}HT_{2C}$ receptors in cerebral cortex and hippocampus showed a significant increase in epileptic rats compared to control rats and *Bacopa monnieri* treated control rats. *Bacopa monnieri* and carbamazepine treatment to epileptic rats reversed the changes to control.

6)   NMDA receptor functional status was analysed by Scatchard analysis using $[^{3}H]$MK-801 in cerebral cortex, hippocampus, cerebellum and brainstem. Receptor gene expression was confirmed by Real-Time PCR. The NMDA receptors were decreased in cerebral cortex and hippocampus while it showed a significant increase in cerebellum and brainstem of epileptic rats compared to

control rats and *Bacopa monnieri* treated control rats. *Bacopa monnieri* and carbamazepine treatment to epileptic rats reversed the changes to control. *Bacopa monnieri* and carbamazepine treatment to epileptic rats reversed the receptor status towards control values.

7) The NMDA2b receptor genes showed down regulation in cerebral cortex, hippocampus while it was up regulated in cerebellum and brainstem of epileptic rats compared to control rats and *Bacopa monnieri* treated control rats. This was reversed to control values with *Bacopa monnieri* and carbamazepine treatment which confirmed the receptor data.

8) The mGLU5 gene was up regulated in cerebral cortex, hippocampus, cerebellum and brainstem of epileptic rats compared to control rats and *Bacopa monnieri* treated control rats. *Bacopa monnieri* and carbamazepine treatment to epileptic rats reversed the changes to near control.

9) The GLAST gene expression was found to be increased in cerebral cortex, hippocampus and brainstem while it was found to be decreased in cerebellum of epileptic rats compared to control rats and *Bacopa monnieri* treated control rats. This was reversed to control values with *Bacopa monnieri* and carbamazepine treatment.

10) The IP3 levels increased significantly in cerebral cortex, hippocampus and brainstem while it decreased significantly in cerebellum of epileptic rats compared to control rats and *Bacopa monnieri* treated control rats. This was reversed to control values with *Bacopa monnieri* and carbamazepine treatment.

11) The cGMP levels increased significantly in hippocampus, cerebellum and brainstem while it showed a significant decrease in cerebral cortex of control rats and *Bacopa monnieri* treated control rats. *Bacopa monnieri* and carbamazepine treatment to epileptic rats reversed the changes to control values.

12) The cAMP levels increased significantly in the cerebral cortex and hippocampus while decreased significantly in cerebellum and brainstem of control rats and *Bacopa monnieri* treated control rats. *Bacopa monnieri* and carbamazepine treatment to epileptic rats reversed the changes to control values.

13) Behavioural studies of the experimental groups of rats were carried out using rotarod test, elevated plus maze test, forced swim test and social interaction test were conducted to assess the changes in the motor and anxiodepressive states.

- The Rotarod experiment demonstrated the impairment in the motor function and coordination in the epileptic rats compared to control rats and *Bacopa monnieri* treated control rats. This was reversed to control values with *Bacopa monnieri* and carbamazepine treatment to epileptic rats.

- Elevated plus maze and social interaction test implicate a role for $5\text{-}HT_{2C}$ receptors in the manifestation of anxiety in the epileptic rats compared to control rats and *Bacopa monnieri* treated control rats. *Bacopa monnieri* treatment to epileptic rats was found to have anxiolytic properties.

- Forced swim test confirmed the depressive traits in the epileptic rats compared to control rats and *Bacopa monnieri* treated control rats. *Bacopa monnieri* and carbamazepine treatment to epileptic rats reversed the alterations to near control.

14) The 5-HT$_{2C}$, NMDA2b and mGlu5 receptor changes in the cerebral cortex and cerebellum were confirmed by confocal studies using receptor specific antibodies in the brain slices.

Our results demonstrate changes in the brain 5-HT$_{2C}$ receptors play a significant role in the motor dysfunction, seizure activity, anxiety and depression during epilepsy. Alterations in the NMDA receptor function lead to seizures, memory and cognitive deficits in brain. *Bacopa monnieri* treatment to epileptic rats significantly reversed these alterations. *Bacopa monnieri* treatment to epileptic rats was effective in neurotransmitter receptor functional regulation in controlling seizures, improving motor function and enhancing the cognitive functions in epileptic rats mediated through 5-HT$_{2C}$ and NMDA receptors. Thus it is evident that *Bacopa monnieri* treatment to epileptic rats renders protection against seizure related excitotoxicity, associated with motor and cognitive deficits. These findings will have clinical significance in the management of epilepsy.

Conclusion

Our findings demonstrated that epilepsy caused significant impact on the central nervous system (CNS) both functionally and behaviourally. The evaluation of these damages at molecular level is very important, especially in the cerebral, hippocampal and cerebellar function. A decrease in the body weight was found in the epileptic group of rats as result of decreased food and water intake. Structural and functional integrity of brain depends on regular glucose and oxygen supply. The receptor binding studies showed alterations in the 5-HT_{2C} and NMDA receptors in the cerebral cortex, hippocampus, cerebellum and brainstem. 5-HT_{2C} receptors were found to be increased in the cerebral cortex and hippocampus while it was decreased in the cerebellum and brainstem of epileptic rats. The NMDA receptors showed a decrease in cerebral cortex and hippocampus while it was significantly increased in brainstem and cerebellum during epilepsy. Real-Time PCR confirmed receptor data of 5-HT_{2C} NMDA2b, mGlu5 and glutamate transporter- GLAST gene expression. The second messenger study confirms that the changes in the receptor levels did percolate through alterations in IP3, cGMP and cAMP levels. These studies suggest that 5-HT_{2C} receptor potentiates Ca^{2+} release through IP3 receptor activation. Also increased NMDA mediated overactivity leading to increased IP3 dependent Ca^{2+} release. Increased Ca^{2+} release triggers release of Cytochrome C thereby initiating the apoptotic process. This causes cell damage during epilepticic stress in the rats. The *Bacopa monnieri* and carbamazepine treatment to epileptic rats is able to reverse this damage. The behavioural studies by rotarod test show a decrease in motor activity in the epileptic rats as result of seizural attack. Epileptic rats suffered from axiogeny and depression which is evident from elevated plus maze test, social interaction test and forced swim test. We showed evidence for dysfunction of the epileptic cerebral cortex and hippocampus that is a reflection for manifestation of abnormal behavioural patterns and possibility for cellular proliferation. The receptor analysis and gene expression studies along with the behavioural data implicate a role for 5-HT_{2C} receptors in the manifestation of anxiety and NMDA receptors for the cognitive and memory deficits associated with epileptic rats. Our findings also suggest dysfunction of the epileptic cerebellum that is a reflection of cerebellar serotonergic and glutamatergic abnormality affecting the motor coordination and timing of action. It is evident that neuroprotective role of *Bacopa monnieri* in epilepsy involves the interaction of 5-HT_{2C} and NMDA receptors, with modulation of mGlu5 and GLAST receptor gene expression at the mRNA level and IP3, cGMP and cAMP activation at the second messenger level. Our experimental results thus support the anticonvulsant property of *Bacopa monnieri* at the molecular level. We conclude from our studies that *Bacopa monnieri* extract treatment potentates a therapeutic effect by reversing the alterations in 5-HT_{2C}, NMDA receptors, mGlu5, GLAST and IP3, cGMP and cAMP that occur during epilepsy, resulting in reduced glutamate-mediated excitotoxity in the brain which has clinical significance in the treatment and management of epilepsy.

References

Abell F, Krams M, Ashburner J, Passingham R, Friston K, Frackowiak R, Happé F, Frith C, Frith U. (1999). The neuroanatomy of autism: A voxel-based whole brain analysis of structural scans. *Neuroreport*, 10: 1647-1651.

Acharya MM, Hattiangady B, Shetty AK. (2008). Progress in neuroprotective strategies for preventing epilepsy. *Progress in Neurobiology*, 84: 363-404.

Adler CM, Goldberg TE, Malhotra AK, Pickar D, Breier A. (1998). Effects of ketamine on thought disorder, working memory, and semantic memory in healthy volunteers. *Biol Psychiatry,* 43: 811-816.

Aithal HN, Sirsi M. (1961). Pharmacological investigation on *Herpestis monniera. Indian J. Pharmacol.*, 23: 2-5.

Alam AM, Starr MS. (1993a). Dopaminergic modulation of pilocarpine-induced motor seizures in the rat: the role of hippocampal D2 receptors. *Neuroscience,* 53: 425-431.

Alam AM, Starr MS. Bimodal. (1994a). Effects of dopamine D2 receptor agonists on zero Mg2+ -induced epileptiform activity in the rat cingulate cortex slice. *Exp. Brain. Res.,* 102: 75-83.

Aldridge JE, Meyer A, Seidler FJ, Slotkin TA. (2005). Alterations in Central Nervous System Serotonergic and Dopaminergic Synaptic Activity in Adulthood after Prenatal or Neonatal Chlorpyrifos Exposure. *Environ. Health Perspect.,* 113: 1027-1031.

Allen G, Buxton RB, Wong EC, Courchesne E. (1997). Attentional activation of the cerebellum independent of motor involvement. *Science*, 275: 1940-1943.

Alonso A, Garcia-Austt E. (1987). Neuronal sources of theta rhythm in the entorhinal cortex of the rat. II. Phase relations between unit discharges and theta field potentials. *Exp. Brain Res.*, 67: 502-509.

Alonso A, Köhler C. (1984). A study of the reciprocal connections between the septum and the entorhinal area using anterograde and retrograde axonal transport methods in the rat brain. *J. Comp. Neurol.*, 225: 327-343.

Altman HJ, Normile HJ, Galloway MP, Ramirez A, Azmita EC. (1990). Enhanced spatial discrimination learning. In rats following 5, 7, DHT- induced serotonergic deafferation of the hippocampus. *Brain Research*, 518: 61-66.

Alves SH, Pinheiro G, Motta V, Landeira-Fernandez J, Cruz APM. (2004). Anxiogenic effects in the rat elevated plus-maze of 5-HT$_{2C}$ agonists into ventral but not dorsal hippocampus. *Behav. Pharmacol.*, 15: 37-43.

Amaducci L, Forno KI, Eng LF. (1981). Glial fibrillary acidic protein in cryogenic lesions of the rat brain. Neuroscience Lett., 21: 27-32.

Amaral DG, Insausti R, Cowan WM. (1983). Evidence for a direct projection from the superior temporal gyrus to the entorhinal cortex in the monkey. *Brain Res.*, 275: 263-277.

Amaral DG, Witter MP. (1989). The three dimensional organization of the hippocampal formation: a review of the anatomical data. *Neuroscience,* 31: 571-591.

Amit DJ, Brunel N, Tsodyks MV. (1994). Correlations of cortical Hebbian reverberations: theory versus experiment. *J. Neurosci.*, 14: 6435-6445.

Applegate CD, Tecott LH. (1998). Global increases in seizure susceptibility in mice lacking 5-HT$_{2C}$ receptors: A behavioural analysis. *Exp. Neurol.*, 154: 522-530.

Arnold PS, Racine RJ, Wise RS. (1973). Effects of atropine, reserpine, 6-hydroxydopamine and handling on seizure development in the rat. *Exp. Neurol.*, 40: 457-470.

Aroniadou-Anderjaska V, Fritsch B, Qashu F, Braga MF. (2008). Pathology and pathophysiology of the amygdala in epileptogenesis and epilepsy. *Epilepsy Res.*, 78: 102-116.

Arriza JL, Eliasof S, Kavanaugh MP, Amara SG. (1997). Excitatory amino acidtransporter 5, a retinal glutamate transporter coupled to a chloride conductance. *Proc. Natl. Acad. Sci. USA*, 94: 4155-4160.

Arriza JL, Fairman WA, Wadiche JI, Murdoch GH, Kavanaugh MP, Amara SG. (1994). Functional comparison of three glutamate transporter subtypes cloned from human motor cortex. *J. Neurosci.*, 14: 5559-5569.

Ashe J, Weimberger NM. (1991). Acetylcholine modulation of cellular excitability via muscarinic receptors: functional plasticity in auditory cortex. *In: Activation and Acquisition: Functional Aspects of the Basal Forebrain Cholinergic System*, edited by R. T. Richardson. Boston: Birkha¨user. 189-246.

Babb TL, Brown WJ, Pretorius JK, Davenport C, Lieb JP, Crandall PH. (1984). Temporal lobe volumetric cell densities in temporal lobe epilepsy. *Epilepsia*, 25: 729-740.

Babb TL, Kupfer WR, Pretorius JK, Isokawa-Akesson M, Levesque MF. (1991). Synaptic recurrent excitation of granule cells by mossy fibers in human epileptic hippocampus. Neuroscience, 42: 351-363.

Babb TL, Pretorius JK, Kupfer WR, Crandall PH. (1989). Glutamate decarboxylase immunoreactive neurons are preserved in human epileptic hippocampus. *J. Neurosci.*, 9: 2562-2574.

Bagdy G, Kecskemeti V, Riba P, Jakus R. (2006). Serotonin and epilepsy. *J. Neurochem.*, 100: 857-873.

Baloh RW, Jacobson KM, Beykirch K, Honrubia V. (1998). Static and dynamic posturography in patients with vestibular and cerebellar lesions. *Arch. Neurol.*, 55: 649-654.

Baltrons AM, Saadoun S, Agullo L, Garcia A. (1997). Regulation of calcium of the nitric oxide/cyclic GMP system in cerebellar granule cells and astroglia in culture. *J. Neurosci. Res.*, 49: 333-341.

Baraban SC, Hollopeter G, Erickson JC, Schwartzkroin PA, Palmiter RD. (1997). Knock-out mice reveal a critical antiepileptic role for neuropeptide Y. *J. Neurosci.*, 17: 8927-8936.

Baran H, Sperk G, Hortnagl H, Sapetschnig G, Hornykiewicz O. (1985). Alpha 2-adrenoceptors modulate kainic acid-induced limbic seizures. *Eur. J. Pharmacol.*, 113: 263-269.

Barnes NM, Sharp T. (1999). A review of central 5-HT receptors and their function. *Neuropharmacology*, 38: 1083-1152.

Bassant MH, Ennouri K, Lamour Y. (1990). Effects of iotophoretically applied monoamines on somatosensory cortical neurons of unanesthetized rats. *Neuroscience*, 39: 431-439.

Bausch SB, Chavkin C. (1997). Changes in hippocampal circuitry after pilocarpineinduced seizures as revealed by opioid receptor distribution and activation. *J. Neuroscience.*, 17: 477-492.

Bausch SB, McNamara JO. (1999). Experimental partial epileptogenesis. Curr.Opin.Neurol., 12: 203-209.

Beck SG, Choi KC. (1991). 5-Hydroxytryptamine hyperpolarizes CA3 hippocampal pyramidal cells through an increase in potassium conductance. *Neurosci. Lett.*, 133: 93-96.

Behr J, Heinemann U. (1996). Effects of serotonin on differnt patterns of low Mg 2+ induced epileptiform activity in the subiculum of rats studied in vitro. *Brain Res.*, 737: 331-334.

Ben-Ari Y. (1985). Limbic seizure and brain damage produced by kainic acid: mechanisms and relevance to human temporal lobe epilepsy. *Neuroscience,* 14: 373-403.

Benquet P, Gee CE, Gerber U. (2002). Two distinct signaling pathways upregulate NMDA receptor responses via two distinct metabotropic glutamate receptor subtypes. *J. Neurosci.*, 22: 9679-9686.

Berridge MJ, Galione A. (1988). Cytosolic calcium oscillators. *FASEB J.*, 15: 3074-3082.

Berridge MJ. (1993). Inositol trisphosphate and calcium signalling. *Nature*, 361:315-325.

Bhattacharya SK, Ghosal S. (1998). Anxiolytic activity of a standardized extract of *Bacopa monniera:* an experimental study. *Phytomedicine*, 5: 77-82.

Bhattacharya SK, Kumar A, Ghosal S. (1999). Effect of *Bacopa monnieri* on animal models of Alzheimer's disease and perturbed central cholinergic markers of cognition in

Bishnoi M, Chopra K, Shrinivas K, Kulkarni. (2008). Protective Effect of L-type Calcium Channel Blockers Against Haloperidol-induced Orofacial Dyskinesia: A Behavioural, Biochemical and Neurochemical Study. *Neurochem. Res.*, 33: 1869-1880.

Bjoras M, Gjesdal O, Erickson JD, Torp R, Levy LM, Ottersen OP, Degree M, Storm-Mathisen J, Seeberg E, Danbolt NC. (1996). Cloning and expression of a neuronal rat brain glutamate transporter. *Mol. Brain Res.*, 36: 163-168.

Bjorklund A, Lindvall O. (1984). Dopamine-containing systems in the CNS. *In: Handbook of Chemical Neuroanatomy:Classical Transmitter in the Rat*, edited by Bjorklund A and Hokfelt T. Amsterdam: Elsevier, 55-122.

Blair RE, Sombati S, Churn SB, Delorenzo RJ. (2008). Epileptogenesis causes an N-methyl-d-aspartate receptor/Ca2+-dependent decrease in Ca2+/calmodulin-dependent protein kinase II activity in a hippocampal neuronal culture model of spontaneous recurrent epileptiform discharges. *Eur. J. Pharmacol.*, 588: 64-71.

Bleakman D, Rusin KI, Chard PS, Glaum SR, Miller RJ. (1992). Metabotropic glutamate receptors potentiate ionotropic glutamate responses in the rat dorsal horn. *Mol. Pharmacol.*, 42: 192-196.

Bliss TVP, Goddard GV, Riives M. (1983). Reduction of long-term potentiation in the dentate gyrus of the rat following selective depletion of monoamines. *J. Physiol.*, 334: 475-491.

Blumer D, Montouris G, Davies K. (2004). The interictal dysphoric disorder: recognition, pathogenesis, and treatment of the major psychiatric disorder of epilepsy. *Epilepsy Behav.*, 5: 826-840.

Bo T, Jiang Y, Cao H, Wang J, Wu X. (2004). Long term effecs of seizures in neonatal rats on spatial learning ability and N-methyl-D-aspartate receptor expression in the brain. *Brain Res. Dev. Brain Res.*152: 137-142.

Boehning D, Patterson RL, Sedaghat L, Glebova NO, Kurosaki T, Snyder SH. (2003). Cytochrome c binds to inositol (1,4,5) trisphosphashate receptors, amplifying calcium-dependant apoptosis. *Nature Cell. Biol.*, 5: 1051-1061.

Boess FG, Martin IL. (1994). Molecular biology of 5-HT receptors. *Neuropharmacology*, 33: 275-317.

Bogdanski DF, Pletscher A, Brodie BB, Udenfriend S. (1956). Identification and assay of serotonin in brain. *J. Pharmacol. Exp. Ther.*, 117: 82-88.

Bonsi P, Cuomo D, De Persis C, Centonze D, Bernardi G, Calabresi P, Pisani A. (2005). Modulatory action of metabotropic glutamate receptor (mGluR) 5 on mGluR1 function in striatal cholinergic interneurons. *Neuropharmacology*, 49: 104-113.

Bootman M, Niggli E, Berridge M, Lipp P. (1997). Imaging the hierarchical Ca2+ signalling system in HeLa cells. *J.Physiol.*, 499: 307-314.

Bordi F, Ugolini A. (1999). Group I metabotropic glutamate receptors: implications for brain diseases. *Prog.Neurobiol.*, 59: 55-79.

Bothwell S, Meredith GE, Phillips J, Staunton H, Doherty C, Grigorenko E, Glazier S, Deadwyler SA, O'Donovan CA, Farrell M. (2001). Neuronal hypertrophy in the neocortex of patients with temporal lobe epilepsy. *J. Neurosci.*, 21: 4789-4800.

Bradford HF. (1995). Glutamate, GABA and epilepsy. *Prog. Neurobiol.*, 47: 477-511.

Bradley PB, Engel G, Feniuk W, Fozard JR, Humphrey PPA, Middlemiss DN, Mylecharane EJ, Richardson BP, Saxena PR. (1986). Proposals for the classification and nomenclature of functional receptors for 5-hydroxytryptamine. *Neuropharmacology*, 25: 563-576.

Bradshaw CM, Sheridan RD, Szabadi E. (1985). Excitatory neuronal responses to dopamine in the cerebral cortex: involvement of D2 but not D1 dopamine receptors. *Brit. J. Pharmacol.*, 86: 483-490.

Bredt DS, Snyder SH. (1990). Isolation of nitric oxide synthetase, a calmodulin-requiring enzyme. *Proc. Natl. Acad. Sci. USA*, 87: 682-685.

Brown I, Martin Smith M. (1960). Anticancer activity of Betulinic acid, a triterpine from *Bacopa monnieri*. *J. Chemi. Soc.*, 2783.

Brusa R, Zimmermann F, Koh DS, Feldmeyer D, Gass P, Seeburg PH, Sprengel R. (1995). Early onset epilepsy and postnatal lethality associated with an editing deficient GluRB allele in mice. *Science*, 270: 1677-1680.

Bunney BS, Aghajanian GK. (1976). Dopamine and norepinephrine innervated cells in the rat prefrontal cortex: pharmacological differentiation using microiontophoretic techniques. *Life Sci.*, 19: 1783-1792.

Burns CM, Chu H, Rueter SM, Hutchinson LK, Canton H, Sanders-Bush E, Emeson RB. (1997). Regulation of Serotonin$_{2C}$ receptor G-protein coupling by RNA editing. *Nature, 387*: 303-308.

Calabrese C, Gregory WL, Leo M, Kraemer D, Bone K, Oken B. (2008). Effects of a Standardized *Bacopa monnieri* Extract on Cognitive Performance, Anxiety, and Depression in the Elderly: A Randomized, Double-Blind, Placebo-Controlled Trial. *J. Altern Complement Med.*, In press.

Campbell BM, Merchant KM. (2003). Serotonin$_{2C}$ receptors within the basolateral amygdala induces acute fear-like responses in an open-field environment. *Brain Res.*, 993: 1-9.

Canaves JM, Taylor SS. (2002).Classification and phylogenetic analysis of the cAMP-dependent protein kinase regulatory subunit family. *J Mol Evol.*, 54: 17-29.

Canton H, Emeson RB, Barker EL, Backstrom JR, Lu JT, Chang MS, Sanders-Bush E. (1996). Identification, molecular cloning, and distribution of a short variant of the 5- hydroxytryptamine$_{2C}$ receptor produced by alternative splicing. *Mol. Pharmacol., 50*: 799-807.

Caramaschi D, de Boer SF, Koolhaas JM. (2007). Differential role of the 5-HT1A receptor in aggressive and non-aggressive mice: an across-strain comparison. *Physiol. Behav.*, 90: 590-601.

Caramanos Z, Shapiro ML. (1994). Spatial memory and N-methyl-D-aspartate receptor antagonists APV and MK-801: memory impairments depend on familiarity with the environment, drug dose, and training duration. Behav Neurosci. 108:30-43.

Carr DB, Cooper DC, Ulrich SL, Spruston ND, Surmeier J. (2002). Serotonin Receptor Activation Inhibits Sodium Current and Dendritic Excitability in Prefrontal Cortex via a Protein Kinase C-Dependent Mechanism. *J. Neurosci.*, 22: 6846-6855.

Castelli F, Frith C, Happe F, Frith U. (2002). Autism, Asperger syndrome and brain mechanisms for the attribution of mental states to animated shapes. *Brain*, 125: 1839-1849.

Cavalheiro EA, Fernandes MJ, Turski L, Naffah-Mazzacoratti MG. (1994). Spontaneous recurrent seizures in rats: amino acid and monoamine determination in the hippocampus. *Epilepsia*, 35: 1-11.

Cavalheiro EA, Leite JP, Bortolotto ZA, Turski WA, Ikonomidou C, Turski L. (1991). Long-term effects of pilocarpine in rats: structural damage of the brain triggers kindling and spontaneous recurrent seizures. *Epilepsia,* 32: 778-782.

Cavazos JE, Golarai G, Sutula TP. (1991). Mossy fiber synaptic reorganization induced by kindling: time course of development, progression, and permanence. *J. Neurosci.*, 11: 2795-2803.

Ceci A, Brambilla A, Duranti P, Grauert M, Grippa N, Borsini F. (1999). Effect of antipsychotic drugs and selective dopaminergic antagonists on dopamineinduced facilitatory activity in prelimbic cortical pyramidal neurons. An in vitro study. *Neuroscience*, 93: 107-115.

Cendelín J, Korelusová I, Vozeh F. (2008). The effect of repeated rotarod training on motor skills and spatial learning ability in Lurcher mutant mice. *Behav. Brain Res.*, 189: 65-74.

Cendes F. (2002). Febrile seizures and mesial temporal sclerosis. *Curr. Opin. Neurol.*, 17: 161-164.

Cepeda C, Li Z, Cromwell HC, Altemus KL, Crawford CA, Nansen EA, Ariano MA, Sibley DR, Peacock WJ, Mathern GW, Levine MS. (1999). Electrophysiological and morphological analyses of cortical neurons obtained from children with catastrophic epilepsy: dopamine receptor modulation of glutamatergic responses. *Dev. Neurosci.,* 21: 223-235.

Cerne R, Randic M. (1992). Modulation of AMPA and NMDA responses in rat spinal dorsal horn neurons by trans-1-aminocyclopentane- 1,3-dicarboxylic acid. *Neurosci. Lett.*, 144: 180-184.

Chakravarty AK, Garai Masuda K, Nakane T, Kawahara N. (2003). *Chem. Phar. Bull.*, 51: 215-217.

Chalmers M, Schell MJ, Thorn P. (2006). Agonist-evoked inositol trisphophate receptor (IP3R) clustering is not dependent on changes in the structure of the endoplasmic reticulum. *Biochem.J.*, 394: 57-66.

Chan-Palay V. (1976). Serotonin axons in the supra- and subependymal plexuses and in the leptomeninges: Their roles in local alterations of cerebrospinal fluid and vasomotor activity. *Brain Res.*, 102: 103-130.

Charriaut-Marlangue C, Ben-Ari Y. (1995). A cautionary note on the use of the TUNEL stain to determine apoptosis. *Neuroreport.*, 7: 61-64.

Chen G, Ensor GR, Bohner B. (1954). A facilitation action of reserpine on the central nervous system. *Proc. Soc. Exp. Biol. Med.*, 86: 507-510.

Chen S, Huang X, Zeng XJ, Sieghart W, Tietz EI. (1999). Benzodiazepine-mediated regulation of alpha1, alpha2, beta1–3 and gamma2 GABA(A) receptor subunit proteins in the rat brain hippocampus and cortex. *Neuroscience*, 93: 33-44.

Chen S, Kobayashi M, Honda Y, Kakuta S, Sato F, Kishi K. (2007). Preferential neuron loss in rat piriform cortex following pilocarpine induced status epilepticus. *Epilepsy Res.*, 74: 1-18.

Cheng Y, Prusoff WH. (1973). Relationship between the inhibition constant (K1) and the concentration of inhibitor which causes 50 per cent inhibition (I50) of an enzymatic reaction. *Biochem. Pharmacol.*, 22: 3099-3108.

Chetkovich DM, Sweatt JD. (1993). NMDA receptor activation increases cyclic AMP in area CA1 of the hippocampus via calcium/calmodulin stimulation of adenylyl cyclase. *J.Neurochem.*, 61: 1933-1942.

Choi DS, Maroteaux L. (1996). Immunohistochemical localisation of the serotonin 5-HT2B receptor in mouse gut, cardiovascular system, and brain. *FEBS Lett.*, 391: 45-51.

Choi DW. (1988). Glutamate neurotoxicity and diseases of the nervous system. *Neuron*, 1: 623-634.

Chu Z, Hablitz JJ. (2000). Quisqualate induces an inward current via mGluR activation in neocortical pyramidal neurons. *Brain Res.*, 879: 88-92.

Clarke WP, Yocca FD, Maayani S. (1996). Lack of 5-hydrotrytamine 1A- mediated inhibition of adenylyl cyclase in dorsal raphe of male and female rats. *J. Pharmacol Exp Ther.*, 277: 1259-1266.

Clifford DB, Olney JW, Maniotis A, Collins RC, Zorumski CF. (1987). The functional anatomy and pathology of lithium-pilocarpine and high-dose pilocarpine seizures. *Neuroscience*, 23: 953-968.

Clinkers R, Gheuens S, Smolders I, Meurs A, Ebinger G, Michotte Y. (2005). *In vivo* modulatory action of extracellular glutamate on the anticonvulsant effects of hippocampal dopamine and serotonin. *Epilepsia*, 46: 828-836.

Cohen, Pitkänen A, Lukasiuk K. (2009). Molecular and cellular basis of epileptogenesis in symptomatic epilepsy. *Epilepsy Behav.*, 14 Suppl 1: 16-25.

Collingridge GL, Bliss TVP. (1987). NMDA receptors-their role in long-term potentiation. *Trends Neurosci.*, 10: 288-293.

Collins JR (1994) Seizures and other neurologic manifestation of allergy. Vet. Clin. North Ann. Small Aim Pract. 24: 735- 748.

Conn PJ, Pin JP. (1997). Pharmacology and function of metabotropic glutamate receptors. *Annu.Rev.Pharmacol.Toxicol.*, 37: 205-237.

Conn PJ, Saunders-Bush E. (1987). Relative efficacies of piperazines at the phosphoinositide hydrolysis-linked serotonergic (5-HT-2 and 5- HT-1c) receptors. *J. Pharmacol. Exp. Ther.*, 242: 552-557.

Conti F, Weinberg RJ. (1999). Shaping excitation at glutamatergic synapses. *Trends Neurosci.*, 22: 451-458.

Conti F, DeBiasi S, Minelli A, Rothstein JD, Melone M. (1998). EAAC1, a high-affinity glutamate tranporter, is localized to astrocytes and gabaergic neurons besides pyramidal cells in the rat cerebral cortex. Cereb Cortex. 8: 108-116.

Corlew R, Brasier DJ, Feldman DE, Philpot BD. (2008). Presynaptic NMDA receptors: newly appreciated roles in cortical synaptic function and plasticity. *Neuroscientist*, 6: 609-625.

Coulter DA, Rafiq A, Shumate M, Gong QZ, DeLorenzo RJ, Lyeth BG. (1996). Brain injury induced enhanced limbic epileptogenesis: anatomical and physiological parallels to an animal model of temporal lobe epilepsy. *Epilepsy Res.*, 26: 81-91.

Covolan L, Mello LE. (2006). Assessment of the progressive nature of cell damage in the pilocarpine model of epilepsy. *Braz. J. Med. Biol. Res.*, 39: 915-924.

Crawley JN. (2007). What's Wrong With My Mouse? Behavioral phenotyping of transgenic and knockout mice, second edition. (John Wiley & Sons, New York).

Cronin J, Obenaus A, Houser CR, Dudek FE. (1992). Electrophysiology of dentate granule cells after kainate-induced synaptic reorganization of mossy fibers. *Brain Res.*, 573: 305-310.

Cryan JF, Holmes A. (2005). The ascent of mouse: advances in modelling human depression and anxiety. *Nat. Rev. Drug Discov.*, 4: 775-790.

Cumming-Hood PA, Strahlendorf HK, Strahlendorf C. (1993). Effects of serotonin and the 5-HT$_{2C/1C}$ receptor agonist. DOl on neurons of the cerebellar dentate/interpositus nuclei: possible involvement of a GABAergic interneuron. *Eur. J. Pharmaco.*, 236: 457-465.

Dailey JW, Jobe PC. (1986). Indices of noradrenergic function in the central nervous system of seizure-naive genetically epilepsy-prone rats. *Epilepsia.*, 27: 665-670.

Dailey JW, Reigel CE, Mishra PK, Jobe PC. (1989). Neurobiology of seizure predisposition in the genetically epilepsy-prone rat. *Epilepsy Res.*, 3: 317-320.

Dailey JW, Reith ME, Yan QS, Li MY, Jobe PC. (1997). Anticonvulsant doses of carbamazepine increase hippocampal extracellular serotonin in genetically epilepsy-prone rats: Dose response relationships. *Neurosci. Lett.*, 227: 13-16.

Danbolt NC, Storm-Mathisen J, Kanner BI. (1992). A [Na1/K1]coupled Lglutamate transporter purified from rat brain is located in glial cell processes. *Neuroscience*, 51: 259-310.

Danbolt NC. (2001). Glutamate uptake. *Prog. Neurobiol.*, 65: 1-105.

Das VA, Finla C, Paulose CS. (2006). Decreased α2 -adrenergic receptor in the brain stem and pancreatic islets during pancreatic regeneration in weanling rats. *Life Sci.*, 79: 1507-1513.

Das A, Shanker G, Nath C, Pal R, Singh S, Singh H. (2002). A comparative study in rodents of standardized extracts of *Bacopa monnieri* and Ginkgo biloba. *Pharmacol.*

Dawson T, Wamseley J. (1983). Autoradiographic localization of [^{3}H]imipramine binding sites: Association with serotonergic neurons. *Brain Res. Bull.*, 11: 325-334.

De Camilli P, Miller PE, Levitt P, Walter U, Greengard P. (1984). Anatomy of cerebellar Purkinje cells in the rat determined by a specific immunohistochemical marker. *Neuroscience*, 11: 761-817.

De Rooij J, Zwartkruis FJ, Verheijen MH, Cool RH, Nijman SM, Wittinghofer A, Bos JL. (1998). Epac is a Rap1 guanine-nucleotide-exchange factor directly activated by cyclic AMP. *Nature*, 396: 474-477.

De Sarro G, Di Paola ED, De Sarro A, Vidai MJ. (1993). L-Arginine potentiates excitatory amino acid-induced seizures elicited in the deep prepiriform cortex. *Eur. J. Pharmacol.*, 230: 151-158.

De Sousa FC, Leite CP, de Melo CT, de Araújo FL, Gutierrez SJ, Barbosa-Filho JM, Fonteles MM, de Vasconcelos, SM, de Barros Viana GS. (2007). Evaluation of effects of N-(2-hydroxybenzoyl) tyramine (riparin II) from Aniba riparia (NEES) MEZ (Lauracea) in anxiety models in mice. *Biol. Pharm. Bull.*, 30: 1212-1216.

De Vente J, Asan E, Gambaryan S, Markerink-van Ittersum M, Axer H, Gallatz K, Lohmann SM, Palkovits M. (2001). Localization of cGMP-dependent protein kinase type II in rat brain. *Neuroscience*, 108: 27-49.

Deacon TW, Eichenbaum H, Rosenberg P, Eckmann KW. (1983). Afferent connections of the perirhinal cortex in the rat. *J. Comp. Neurol.*, 220: 168-190.

Deepak M, Amit A. (2004). The need for establishing identities of 'bacoside A and B', the putative major bioactive saponins of Indian medicinal plant *Bacopa monnieri. Phytomedicine*, 11: 264-268.

Degiorgio CM, Tomiyasu U, Gott PS, Treiman DM. (1992). Hippocampal pyramidal cell loss in human status epilepticus. *Epilepsia*, 33: 23-27.

Dekeyne A, Mannoury la Cour C, Gobert A, Brocco M, Lejeune F, Serres F, Sharp T, Daszuta A, Soumier A, Papp M, Rivet JM, Flik G, Cremers TI, Muller O, Lavielle G, Millan MJ. (2008). S32006, a novel 5-HT$_{2C}$ receptor antagonist displaying broad- based antidepressant and anxiolytic properties in rodent models. *Psychopharmacology*, 199: 549-568.

Delgado PL. (2004). Common pathways of depression and pain. *J. Clin. Psychiatry*, 65: S16-S19.

Descarries L, Beaudet A, Watkins K. (1975). Serotonin nerve terminals in adult rat neocortex. *Brain Res.*, 100: 563-588.

Devinsky O. (2004). Diagnosis and treatment of temporal lobe epilepsy. *Rev. Neurol. Dis.*, 1: 2-9.

Dhawan BN, Singh HK. (1996). Pharmacological studies on *Bacopa monniera*, an Ayurvedic nootropic agent. *European Journal of Neuropsychopharmacology*, 653: 144-149.

Dieudonné S, Dumoulin A. (2000). Serotonin-Driven Long-Range Inhibitory Connections in the Cerebellar Cortex. *Journal of Neurosci.*, 20: 1837-1848.

Di Giovanni G, Di Matteo V, Pierucci M, Benigno A, Esposito E. (2006). Central serotonin$_{2C}$ receptor: from physiology to pathology. *Curr.Topics Med.Chem.*, 6: 1909-1925.

Dichter MA. (1994). Emerging insights into mechanisms of epilepsy: implications for new antiepileptic drug development. *Epilepsia.*, 35: 51-57.

Dickson CT, Alonso A. (1997). Muscarinic induction of synchronous population activity in the entorhinal cortex. *J. Neurosci.*, 17: 6729-6744.

Dickson CT, Kirk IJ, Oddie SD, Bland BH. (1995). Classification of theta-related cells in the entorhinal cortex: cell discharges are controlled by the ascending brainstem synchronizing pathway in parallel with hippocampal theta-related cells. *Hippocampus,* 5: 306-319.

Diener H, Dichgans J, Guschlbauer B, Bacher M, Langenbach P. (1989). Disturbances of motor preparation in basal ganglia and cerebellar disorders. *Prog. Brain Res.*, 80: 481-488.

Ding D, Hong Z, Wang WZ, Wu JZ, de Boer HM, Prilipko L, Sander JW. (2006). Assessing the disease burden due to epilepsy by disability adjusted life year in rural China. *Epilepsia*, 47: 2032-2037.

Dingledine R, Borges K, Bowie D, Traynelis SF. (1999). The glutamate receptor ion channels. *Pharmacol. Rev.*, 51: 07-61.

Dremier S, Pohl V, Poteet-Smith C, Roger PP, Corbin J, Doskeland SO, Dumont JE, Maenhaut C. (1997). Activation of cyclic AMP-dependent kinase is required but may not be sufficient to mimic cyclic AMP-dependent DNA synthesis and thyroglobulin expression in dog thyroid cells. *Mol. Cell Biol.*, 11: 6717-6726.

Duan YHL, Wu CM, Shen CL. (1989). Distribution of serotonin immunoreactive neurons in the brainstem of the hamster, guinea pig, rabbit and rat. *Proc. Natl. Sci. Conc. Repub. China B*, 13: 218-219.

Dunham NW, Miya TS. (1957). A Note on a Simple Apparatus for Detecting Neurological Deficit in Rats & Mice. *J. Am. Pharmaceut. Assoc. Scientific Edit*, XLVI: No. 3.

Dunnett S, Fibiger HC. (1993). Role of forebrain cholinergic systems in learning and memory: relevance to the cognitive deficits of aging and Alzheimer's dementia. *Prog. Brain Res.*, 98: 413-420.

Durstewitz D, Seamans JK, Sejnowski TJ. (2000). Dopamine-mediated stabilization of delay-period activity in a network model of prefrontal cortex. *J. Neurophysiol.*, 83: 1733-1750.

Dutton AC, Barnes NM. (2006). Anti-obesity pharmacotherapy: future perspectives utilising 5-HT$_{2C}$ receptor agonists. *Drug Disc Today: Therapeutic Strategies*, 3: 577-583.

Ekonomou A, Angelatou F. (1999). Upregulation of NMDA receptors in hippocampus and cortex in the pentylenetetrazol-induced "kindling" model of epilepsy. *Neurochem. Res.*, 24: 1515-1522.

Elangovan V, Govindasamy S, Ramamoorthy N, Balasubramanian K. (1995). In vitro studies on the anticancer activity of *Bacopa monnieri*. *Fitoterapia*, 11: 66-211.

Endoh T. (2004). Characterization of modulatory effects of postsynaptic metabotropic glutamate receptors on calcium currents in rat nucleus tractus solitarius. *Brain Res.*, 1024: 212-224.

Engel J. Jr. (1996). Introduction to temporal lobe epilepsy. *Epilepsy Res.*, 26: 141-150.

Engel J. Jr. (2001). Intractable epilepsy: definition and neurobiology. *Epilepsia*, 42 Suppl. (6), 3.

Erecińska M, Silver IA. (1992). Relationship between ions and energy metabolism: cerebral calcium movements during ischemia and subsequent recovery. *Can. J. Physiol. Pharmacol.*, 70: 190-193.

Erickson JC, Clegg KE, Palmiter RD. (1996). Sensitivity to leptin and susceptibility to seizures of mice lacking neuropeptide Y. *Nature*, 381: 415-421.

Erlander MG, Lovenberg TW, Baron BM, De Lecea L, Danielson PE, Racke M, Slone AL, Siegel BW, Foye PE, Cannon K. (1993). Two members of a distinct subfamily of 5-hydroxytryptamine receptors differentially expressed in rat brain. *Proc. Natl. Acad. Sci.*, 90: 3452-3456.

Ernst E. (2006). Herbal remedies for anxiety - a systematic review of controlled clinical trials. Phytomedicine. 13: 205-208.

Eskandari S, Kreman M, Kavanaugh MP, Wright EM, Zampighi GA. (2000). Pentameric assembly of a neuronal glutamate transporter. *Proc Natl Acad Sci. U S A*. 97:8641-8646.

Esclapez M, Hirsch JC, Ben-Ari Y, Bernard C. (1999). Newly formed excitatory pathways provide a substrate for hyperexcitability in experimental temporal lobe epilepsy. *J. Comp. Neurol.*, 408: 449-460.

Faingold CL (1999). Neurons in the deep layers of superior colliculus play a critical role in the neuronal network for audiogenic seizures: mechanisms for production of wild running behavior. *Brain Res.*, 815: 250-258.

Fairman WA, Vandenberg RJ, Arriza JL, Kavanaugh MP, Amara SG. (1995). An excitatory amino-acid transporter with properties of a ligand-gated chloride channel. *Nature*, 375: 599-603.

Feldman S. and Weidenfeld J. (1998). The excitatory effect of amygdala on hypothalamo pituitary adrenocortical responses are mediated by hypothalamic norepinephrine, serotonin, and CRF-41. Brain Research Bulletin, 45: 389-93.

Ferron A, Thierry AM, LeDouarin C, Glowinski J. (1984). Inhibitory influence of the mesocortical dopaminergic system on spontaneous activity or excitatory response induced from the thalamic mediodorsal nucleus in the rat medial prefrontal cortex. *Brain Res.*, 302: 257-265.

Fiscus RR, Rapoport RM, Waldman SA, Murad F. (1985). Atriopeptin II elevates cyclic GMP, activates cyclic GMP-dependent protein kinase and causes relaxation in rat thoracic aorta. *Biochem.Biophys.Acta.*, 846: 179-184.

Fisher PD, Sperber EF, Moshe SL. (1998). Hippocampal sclerosis revisited. *Brain Dev.*, 20: 563-573.

Fletcher A, Forster EA. (1988). A proconvulsant action of selective a2-adrenoceptor antagonists. *Eur. J. Pharmacol.*, 151: 27-34.

Fone KC, Shalders K, Fox ZD, Arthur R, Marsden CA. (1996). Increased 5-HT$_{2C}$ receptor responsiveness occurs on rearing rats in social isolation. *Psychopharmacology*, 123: 346-352.

Fone KCF, Austin RH, Topham IA, Kennett GA, Punhani T. (1998). Effect of chronic *m*-CPP on locomotion, hypophagia, plasma corticosterone and 5-HT$_{2C}$ receptor levels in the rat. *Br. J. Pharmacol.*, 123: 1707-1715.

Fone KCF, Shalders K, Fox ZD, Arthur R, Marsden CA. (1996). Increased 5-HT$_{2C}$ receptor responsiveness occurs on rearing rats in social isolation. *Psychopharmacologia*, 23: 346-352.

Freitas RM, Sousa FC, Viana GS, Fonteles MM. (2006). Effect of gabaergic, glutamatergic, antipsychotic and antidepressant drugs on pilocarpine-induced seizures and status epilepticus. Neurosci.Lett., 408: 79-83.

Frotscher M, Zimmer J. (1983). Lesion-induced mossy fibers to the molecular layer of the rat fascia dentata: identification of postsynaptic granule cells by the Golgi-EM technique. *J Comp Neurol*, 215 : 299-311.

Fujii S, Sasaki H, Mikoshiba K, Kuroda Y, Yamazaki Y, Mostafa Taufiq A, Kato H. (2004). A chemical LTP induced by co-activation of metabotropic and N-methyl-D-aspartate glutamate receptors in hippocampal CA1 neurons. *Brain Res.*, 999: 20-28.

Funahashi S, Bruce CJ, Goldman-Rakic PS.(1989). Mnemonic coding of visual space in the monkey's dorsolateral prefrontal cortex. *J. Neurophysiol.*, 61: 331-349.

Fuxe K, Calza L, Benfenati F, Zini I, Agnatti L. (1983). Quantitative autoradiographic localization of [3H]imipramine binding sites in the brain of the rat. Relationship to ascending 5-hydroxytryptamine neuron systems. *Proc. Natl. Acad. Sci. USA*, 80: 3836-3840.

Gall CM, lsackson PJ. (1989). Limbic seizures increase neuronal production of messenger RNA for nerve growth factor. *Science*, 245: 758-761.

Galván EJ, Calixto E, Barrionuevo G. (2008). Bidirectional Hebbian plasticity at hippocampal mossy fiber synapses on CA3 interneurons. *J.Neurosci.*, 28: 14042-55.

Garthwaite J. (1991). Glutamate, nitric oxide and cell-cell signaling in the nervous system. *Trends Neurosci.*, 14: 60-67.

Garthwaite J. (2005). Dynamics of cellular NO-cGMP signaling. *Front. Biosci.*, 10: 1868-1880.

Gastens Alexandra M, Brandt Claudia, Bankstahl JP, Löscher Wolfgang. (2008). Predictors of pharmacoresistant epilepsy: Pharmacoresistant rats differ from pharmacoresponsive rats in behavioral and cognitive abnormalities associated with experimentally induced epilepsy. Epilepsia, 49: 1759-1776.

Gaykema RPA, Luiten PGM, Nyakas C, Traber J. (1990). Cortical projection patterns of the medial septum-diagonal band complex. *J. Comp. Neurol.,* 293: 103-124.

Geijo-Barrientos E, Pastore C. (1995). The effects of dopamine on the sub threshold electrophysiological responses of rat prefrontal cortex neurons in vitro. *Eur. J. Neurosci.,* 7: 358-366.

George B, Kulkarni SK. (1997). Modulation of lithium-pilocarpine-induced status epilepticus by adenosinergic agents. *Methods Find Exp. Clin. Pharmacol.,* 19: 329-333.

Giorgetti M, Tecott LH. (2004). Contributions of 5-HT_{2C} receptors to multiple actions of central serotonin systems. *Eur. J. Pharmacol.,* 488: 1-9.

Glowinski J, Iversen LL. (1966). Regional studies of catecholamines in the rat brain: The disposition of [3H] Norepinephrine, [3H] DOPA in various regions of the brain. *J. Neurochem.,* 13: 655-669.

Gobert A, Rivet J, Lejeune F, Newman-Tancredi A, Adhumeau-Auclair A, Nicolas JP. (2000). Serotonin(2C) receptors tonically suppress the activity of mesocortical dopaminergic and adrenergic, but not serotonergic pathways, a combined dialysis and electrophysiological analysis in the rat. *Synapse,* 36: 205-221.

Gold PW. (2005). The neurobiology of stress and its relevance to psychotherapy. Clinical *Neuroscience Research,* 4: 315–324.

Gonzalez MI, Ortega A. (2000). Regulation of high-affinity glutamate uptake activity in Bergmann glia cells by glutamate. *Brain Res.,* 866: 73-81.

Gonzalez-Burgos G, Kroner S, Krimer LS, Seamans JK, Urban NN, Henze DA, Lewis DA, Barrionuevo G. (2002). Dopamine modulation of neuronal function in the monkey prefrontal cortex. *Physiol. Behav.,* 77: 537-543.

Gonzalez-Islas C, Hablitz JJ. (2003). Dopamine enhances EPSCs in layer II-III pyramidal neurons in rat prefrontal cortex. *J. Neurosci.,* 23: 867-875.

Gorelova N, Yang CR. (2000). Dopamine D1/D5 receptor activation modulates a persistent sodium current in rat prefrontal cortical neurons *in vitro*. *J. Neurophysiol.*, 84: 75-87.

Goulding EH, Ngai J, Kramer RH, Colicos S, Axel R, Siegelbaum SA, Chess, A. (1992). Molecular cloning and single-channel properties of the cyclic nucleotide-gated channel from catfish olfactory neurons. Neuron, 8: 45-58.

Gowen E, Miall C. (2005). Behavioural aspects of cerebellar function in adults with Asperger syndrome. *The Cerebellum*, 4: 1-11.

Grailhe R, Amlaiky AN, Ghavami A, Ramboz S, Yocca F, Mahle C, Margouris C, Perrot F, Hen R. (1994). Human and mouse 5-HT5A and 5-HT5B receptors: Cloning and functional expression. *Soc. Neurosci. Abstr.*, 20: 1160.

Graumlich, JF, Mc Laughlin RG, Birkhahn D, Shah N, Jobe, PC, Dailey JW. (1999). Carbamazepine pharmacokinetics-pharmacodynamics in genetically epilepsy-prone rats. *Eur. J. Pharmacol.*, 369: 305-311.

Grigorenko E, Glazier S, Bell W, Tytell M, Nosel E, Pons T, Deadwyler SA. (1997). Changes in glutamate receptor subunit composition in hippocampus and cortex in patients with refractory epilepsy. *J. Neurol. Sci.*, 153: 35-45.

Gulledge AT, Jaffe DB. (2001). Multiple effects of dopamine on layer V pyramidal cell excitability in rat prefrontal cortex. *J. Neurophysiol.*, 86: 586-595.

Gurevich I, Tamir H, Arango V, Dwork AJ, Mann JJ, Schmauss G. (2002). Altered editing of Serotonin 2C receptor pre-mRNA in the prefrontal cortex of depressed suicide victims. *Neuron*, 34: 349-356.

Guzman HDP, Inaba Y, Baldelli E, de Curtis M, Biagini G, Avoli M. (2008). Network hyperexcitability within the deep layers of pilocarpine-treated rat entorhinal cortex. *J Physiol.*, 586:1867-83.

Hackler EA, Turner GH, Gresch PJ, Sengupta S, Deutch AY, Avison MJ, Gore JC, Sanders-Bush E. (2007). 5-Hydroxytryptamine2C receptor contribution to m-chlorophenylpiperazine and N-methylb- carboline-3-carboxamide-induced anxiety-like behavior and limbic brain activation. *J. Pharm. Exp. Ther.*, 320: 1023-1029.

Hagan JJ, Hatcher JP, Slade PD. (1995). The role of 5-HT1D and 5-HT1A receptors in mediating 5-hydroxytryptophan induced myoclonic jerks in guinea pigs. *Eur.*

J. Pharmacol., 294: 743-751.

Hajnal A, Lenard L, Czurko A, Sandor P, Karadi Z. (1997). Distribution and time course of appearance of 'dark' neurons and EEG activity after amygdaloid kainate lesion. *Brain Res. Bull.,* 433: 235-243.

Hajszan T, MacLusky NJ. (2006). Neurologic links between epilepsy and depression in women: is hippocampal neuroplasticity the key? *Neurology*, 66: S13-S22.

Hamon M, Bourgoin S, el Mestikawy S, Goetz C. (1982). Central serotonin receptors. *Oxford: Blackwell Science*: 107-143.

Hardman JG, Goodman Gilman A, Limbird LE. (1996). *Goodman & Gilman's The Pharmacological Basis of Therapeutics. New York, New York: McGraw- Hill,* 237-365.

Harvey AS, Berkovic SF, Wrennall JA, Hopkins IJ. (1997). Temporal lobe epilepsy in childhood: clinical, EEG, and neuroimaging findings and syndrome classification in a cohort with new-onset seizures. *Neurology*, 49: 960-968.

Hashimoto Y, Araki H, Gomita Y. (2004). Cessation of repeated administration of MK-801 changes the anticonvulsant effect against flurothyl-induced seizure in mice. *Pharmacol. Biochem. Behav.*, 74: 909-915.

Hauser WA. (1997). Incidence and prevalence. In: Engel JJr, Pedley TA (eds). Epilepsy – A Comprehensive Textbook. *Lippincott-Raven Publishers, Philadephia*, 47-58.

Heffner TG, Hartman JA, Seiden LS. (1980). A rapid method for the regional dissection of the rat brain. *Pharmacol. Biochem. Behav.*, 13: 453-456.

Heiser LK, Chu HM, Tecott LH. (1998). Epilepsy and obesity in serotonin 5-HT$_{2C}$ receptor mutant mice. *Ann. N.Y. Acad. Sci.*, 861: 74-78.

Hellier JL, White A, Williams PA, Edward Dudek F, Staley KJ. (2009). NMDA receptor-mediated long-term alterations in epileptiform activity in experimental chronic epilepsy. *Neuropharmacology*, In press.

Henze DA, Lewis DA, Barrionuevo G. (2002). Dopamine modulation of neuronal function in the monkey prefrontal cortex. *Physiol. Behav.*, 77: 537-543.

Hernandez EJ, Willams PA, Dudek FE. (2002). Effect of fluoxetine and TFMPP on spontaneous seizures in rats with pilocarpine induced epilepsy. *Epilepsia.*, 43: 1337-1345.

Herrick-Davis K, Grinde E, Niswender CM. (1999). Serotonin 5-HT$_{2C}$ receptor RNA editing alters receptor basal activity: implications for serotonergic signal transduction. *J. Neurochem.*, 73: 1711-1717.

Hertz L, Dringen R, Schousboe A, Robinson SR. (1999). Astrocytes: glutamate producers for neurons. *J. Neurosci. Res.*, 57: 417-428.

Heslop KE, Curzon G. (1999). Effect of reserpine on behavioural responses to agonists at 5-HT$_{1A}$, 5-HT$_{1B}$, 5-HT$_{2A}$, and 5-HT$_{2C}$ receptor subtypes. *Neuropharmacology,* 38: 883-891.

Ho BC, Mola C, Andreasen NC. (2004). Cerebellar dysfunction in neuroleptic naive schizophrenia patients: Clinical, cognitive, and neuroanatomic correlates of cerebellar neurologic signs. *Biol. Psychiatry*, 55: 1146-1153.

Hoffman DJ, Zanelli SA, Kubin JM, Om P, Delivoria-P, Maria. (1996). The *in vivo* Effect of Bilirubin on theN-Methyl-D-Aspartate Receptor/Ion Channel Complex in the Brains of Newborn Piglets. *Ped. Res.*, 40: 804-808.

Holmes A, Rodgers RJ. (1998). Responses of Swiss-Webster mice to repeated plus-maze experience: further evidence for a qualitative shift in emotional state? *Pharmacol. Biochem. Behav.*, 60: 473-488.

Holmes GL. (2006). Clinical evidence that epilepsy is a progressive disorder with special emphasis on epilepsy syndromes that do progress. *Adv. Neurol.*, 97: 323-331.

Holmes KH, Keele NB, Shinnick-Gallagher P. (1996). Loss of mGluR-mediated hyperpolarizations and increase in mGluR depolarizations in basolateral amygdala neurons in kindling-induced epilepsy. *J. Neurophysiol.*, 76: 2808-2812.

Holmes MD, Silbergeld DL, Drouhard D,Wilensky AJ, Ojemann LM. (2004). Effect of vagus nerve stimulation on adults with pharmacoresistant generalized epilepsy syndromes. *Seizure*, 13: 340-345.

Holopainen I, Louve M, Enkvist MO, Akerman KE. (1989). 86Rubidium release from cultured primary astrocytes: effects of excitatory and inhibitory amino acids. Neuroscience. 30:223-229.

Holopainen I, Louve M, Enkvist MOK, Akerman KEO. (1990). Coupling of glutamatergic receptors to changes in intracellular Ca2+ in rat cerebellar granule cells in primary culture. *J. Neurosci. Res.*, 25: 187-193.

Horii Y, Yamasaki N, Miyakawa T, Shiosaki S. (2008). Increased anxiety-like behavior in neuropsin (kallikrein-related peptidase 8) gene-deficient mice. *Behav. Neurosci.*, 122: 498-504.

Houser CR. (1990). Granule cell dispersion in the dentate gyrus of humans with temporal lobe epilepsy. *Brain Res.*, 535: 195-204.

Hoyer D, Martin G. (1997). 5-HT receptor classification and nomenclature: Towards a harmonization with the human genome. *Neuropharmacology*, 36: 419-428.

Hoyer D, Clarke DE, Fozard JR, Hartig PR, Martin GR, Mylecharane EJ, Saxena PR, Humphrey PPA. (1994). International Union for Pharmacology classification of receptors for 5-Hydroxytryptamine (Serotonin). *Pharmacol. Rev.*, 46: 157-203.

Huerta PT, Lisman JE. (1993). Heightened synaptic plasticity of hippocampal CA1 neurons during a cholinergically induced rhythmic state. *Nature*, 19: 723-725.

Humphrey PPA, Hartig, P, Hoyer D. (1993). A proposed new nomenclature for 5-HT receptors. *Trends Pharmacol. Sci.*, 14: 233-236.

Hutson PH, Barton CL, Jay M. Blurton P, Burkamp F, Clarkson R, Bristow LJ. (2000). Activation of mesolimbic dopamine function by phencyclidine is enhanced by 5-HT$_{(2C/2B)}$ receptor antagonists, neurochemical and behavioural studies. *Neuropharmacology*, 39: 2318-2328.

Hyyppa M, Wurtman RJ. (1973). Biogenic amines in the pituitary gland: what is their origin and function? Pituitary indolamines. *Prog. Brain Res.*, 39: 211-215.

Imazumi H, Miyauchi S, Tamada T, Sasaki Y, Takino R, Futz B, Yoshioka T, Kawato M. (2004). Human cerebellar activity reflecting an acquired internal model of a new tool. *Nature*, 3: 192-195.

Insausti R, Amaral DG, CowanWM. (1987). The entorhinal cortex of the monkey: II. Cortical afferents. *J. Comp. Neurol.*, 264: 356-395.

Insausti R, Herrero MT, Witter MP. (1997). Entorhinal cortex of the rat: cytoarchitectonic subdivisions and the origin and distribution of cortical efferents. *Hippocampus,* 7: 146-183.

Isokawa M, Mello LE. (1991). NMDA receptor-mediated excitability in dendritically deformed dentate granule cells in pilocarpine-treated rats. *Neurosci. Lett.,* 129: 69-73.

Isokawa M. (1996). Decreased time constant in hippocampal dentate granule cells in pilocarpine treated rats with progressive seizure frequencies. *Brain Res.,* 718: 169-175.

Isokawa M. (1998). Remodeling dendritic spines in the rat pilocarpine model of temporal lobe epilepsy. *Neuroscience Lett.,* 258: 73-76.

Ivry R, Keele SW, Diener HC. (1988). Dissociation of the lateral and medial cerebellum in movement timing and movement execution. *Exp. Brain Res.,* 73: 167-180.

Jackson HC, Dickinson SL, Nutt DJ. (1991). Exploring the pharmacology of the proconvulsant effects of alpha 2-adrenoceptor antagonists in mice. *Psychopharmacology,* 105: 558-562.

Jackson J, Paulose CS. (1999). Enhancement of [m-methoxy 3H]MDL100907 binding to 5HT2A receptors in cerebral cortex and brain stem of streptozotocin induced diabetic rats. *Mol. Cell. Biochem.,* 199: 81-85.

Jacobs B, Azmitia E. (1992). Structure and function of the brain serotonin system. *Physiol. Rev.,* 72: 165-229.

Jacobs BL, Fornal CA. (1997). Serotonin and motor activity. *Curr. Opin. Neurobiol.,* 7: 820-825.

Jancke L, Loose R, Lutz K, Specht K, Shah NJ. (2000). Cortical activations during paced finger-tapping applying visual and auditory pacing stimuli. *Brain Res. Cogn. Brain Res.,* 10: 51-66.

Janigro D. (2008). Gene expression in temporal lobe epilepsy. *Epilepsy Currents,* 8: 23-24.

Javitt DC, Steinschneider M, Schroeder CE, Arezzo JC. (1996). Role of cortical N-methyl-D-aspartate receptors in auditory sensory memory and mismatch negativity generation: implications for schizophrenia. *Proc. Natl. Acad. Sci. U.S.A.*, 1593: 11962-11967.

Jerlicz M, Kostowski W, Bidzi'nski A, Hauptman M, Dymecki J. (1978). Audiogenic seizures in rats: relation to noradrenergic neurons of the locus coeruleus. *Acta. Physiol. Pol.*, 29: 409-412.

Jobe PC, Ko KH, Dailey JW. (1984). Abnormalities in norepinephrine turnover rate in the central nervous system of the genetically epilepsy prone rat. *Brain Res.*, 290: 357-360.

Jocobs BL, Azimitia EC. (1992). Structure and function of the brain serotonin system. *Physio. Rev.*, 72: 165-229.

Johnson EW, deLanerolle NC, Kim JH. (1992). Central and peripheral benzodiazepine receptors: opposite changes in human epileptogenic tissue. *Neurology*, 42: 811-815.

Jones EG, Powell TPS. (1970). An anatomical study of converging sensory pathways within the cerebral cortex of the monkey. *Brain*, 93: 793-820.

Jouvert P, Revel MO, Lazaris A, Aunis D, Langley K, Zwiller J. (2004). Activation of the GMP Pathway in Dopaminergic Structures Reduces Cocaine-Induced EGR-1 Expression and Locomotor Activity. *J. Neuroscience*, 24: 10716-10725.

Julius D, Livelli TJ, Jessell TM, Axel R. (1989). Ectopic expression of the serotonin 1c receptor and the triggering of malignant transformation. *Science*, 244: 1057-1062.

Julius D, MacDermott AB, Axel R, Jessel TM. (1988). Molecular characterization of a functional cDNA encoding the serotonin 1c receptor. *Science*, 241: 558-564.

Jyoti A, Sharma D. (2004). Neuroprotective role of *Bacopa monniera* extract against aluminium-induced oxidative stress in the hippocampus of rat brain. *Neurotoxicology*, 27: 451-457.

Kalia LV, Kalia SK, Salter MW. (2008). NMDA receptors in clinical neurology: excitatory times ahead. *Lancet Neurol.*, 7: 742-755.

Kalisch R, Holt B, Petrovic P, De Martino B, Klöppel S, Büchel C, Dolan RJ. (2009). The NMDA agonist D-cycloserine facilitates fear memory consolidation in humans. *Cereb.Cortex*, 19: 187-96.

Kanai Y, Smith CP, Hediger MA. (1993). The elusive transporters with a high affinity for glutamate. *Trends Neurosci.*, 16: 365-370.

Kanai Y, Hediger MA. (1992). Primary structure and functional characterization of a high-affinity glutamate transporter. *Nature*. 360:467-471.

Kanai Y, Bhide PG, DiFiglia M, Hediger MA. (1995). Neuronal high-affinity glutamate transport in the rat central nervous system. *Neuroreport.* 6: 2357-2362.

Kandel A, Buzsaki G. (1993). Cerebellar neuronal activity correlates with spike and wave EEG patterns in the rat. *Epilepsy Res.*, 16: 1-9.

Kanner AM. (2006). Depression and epilepsy: a new perspective on two closely related disorders. *Epilepsy Curr.*, 6: 141-146.

Kanner BI, Schuldiner S. (1987). Mechanism of transport and storage of neurotransmitters. *CRC Crit. Rev. Biochem.*, 22: 1-38.

Kao CQ, Coulter DA. (1997). Physiology and pharmacology of corticothalamic stimulation-evoked responses in rat somatosensory thalamic neurons in vitro. *J. Neurophysiol.*, 77: 2661-2676.

Kapur J, Michelson HB, Buterbaugh GG, Lothman EW. (1989). Evidence for a chronic loss of inhibition in the hippocampus after kindling: electrophysiological studies. *Epilepsy Res.,* 4: 90-99.

Kapur J. (1999). Status epilepticus in epileptogenesis. *Curr. Opin. Neurol.*, 12: 191-195.

Karlin A, Akabas MH. (1995). Toward a structural basis for the function of nicotinic acetylcholine receptors and their cousins. *Neuron*, 15: 1231-1244.

Kaufman MJ, Hartig PR, Hoffman BJ. (1995). Serotonin 5-HT$_{2C}$ receptor stimulates cyclic GMP formation in choroid plexus. *J. Neurochem.*, 64: 199-205.

Kaupp UB, Niidome T, Tanabe T, Terada S, Bönigk W, Stühmer W, Cook NJ, Kangawa K, Matsuo H, Hirose T. (1989). Primary structure and functional expression from complementary DNA of the rod photoreceptor cyclic GMP-gated channel. *Nature*, 342: 762-766.

Kawasaki H, Springett GM, Mochizuki N, Toki S, Nakaya M, Matsuda M, Housman DE, Graybiel AM. (1998). A family of cAMP-binding proteins that directly activate Rap1. *Science*, 282: 2275-2259.

Keele NB. (2001). Phenytoin inhibits isolation-induced aggression specifically in rats with low serotonin. *Neuroreport*, 12: 1107-12.

Kerr JF, Wyllie AH, Curre AR. (1972). Apoptosis: a basic biological phenomenon with wide ranging implications in tissue kinetics. *Br. J. Cancer.*, 26: 239-257.

Kishore K, Singh M. (2005). Effect of bacosides, alcoholic extract of *Bacopa monnieri* Linn. (brahmi), on experimental amnesia in mice. *Indian J. Exper. Biol.*, 43: 640-645.

Klein DC, Coon SL, Roseboom PH, Weller JL, Bernard M, Gastel JA, Zazt M, Iuvone PM, Rodriguez IR, Begay V, Falcon J, Cahill GM, Cassone VM, Baler R. (1997). The melatonin rhythm-generating enzyme: molecular regulation of serotonin N-acetyltransferase in the pineal gland. *Recent Prog. Horm. Res.*, 52: 307-358.

Klink R, Alonso A. (1997). Muscarinic modulation of the oscillatory and repetitive firing properties of entorhinal cortex layer II neurons. *J. Neurophysiol.*, 77: 1813-1828.

Kohen R, Metcalf MA, Khan N, Druck T, Huebner K, Lachowicz JE, Meltzer HY, Sibley DR, Roth BL, Hamblin MW. (1996). Cloning, characterization, and chromosomal localization of a human 5-HT6 serotonin receptor. *J. Neurochem.*, 66: 47-56.

Kohler C. (1986). Intrinsic connections of the retrohippocampal region in the rat brain. II. The medial entorhinal area. *J. Comp. Neurol.*, 246: 149-169.

Kohr G, Lambert CE, Mody I. (1991). Calbindin-D28K (CaBP) levels and calcium currents in acutely dissociated epileptic neurons. *Exp. Brain Res.*, 85: 543-551.

Kolb TF, Lachauer S, Schoch B, Gerwig M, Timmann D, Kolb FP. (2007). Comparison of the electrically evoked leg withdrawal reflex in cerebellar patients and healthy controls. *Exp. Brain Res.*, 177: 493-508.

Komada M, Saitsu H, Kinboshi M, Miura T, Shiota K, Ishibashi M. (2008). Hedgehog signaling is involved in development of the neocortex. *Development.* 135: 2717-2727.

Kondziella Daniel, Alvestad Silje, Vaaler Arne, Sonnewald Ursula. (2007). Which clinical and experimental data link temporal lobe epilepsy with depression? *Journal of Neurochemistry*, 103: 2136–2152.

Koob GF, Heinrichs SC. (1999). A role for corticotropin releasing factor and urocortin in behavioral responses to stressors. *Brain Res.*, 848:141-52.

Kotecha SA, Jackson MF, Al-Mahrouki A, Roder JC, Orser BA, MacDonald JF. (2003). Co-stimulation of mGluR5 and N-methyl- D-aspartate receptors is required for potentiation of excitatory synaptic transmission in hippocampal neurons. *J. Biol. Chem.*, 278: 27742-27749.

Krnjevi´c K. (1993). Central cholinergic mechanisms and function. *Prog. Brain Res.*, 98: 285-292.

Krystal JH, Karper LP, Seibyl JP, Freeman GK, Delaney R, Bremner JD. (1994). Subanesthetic effects of the noncompetitive NMDA antagonist, ketamine, in humans: psychotomimetic, perceptional, cognitive and neuroendocrine response. *Arch. Gen. Psychiatry*, 51: 199-214.

Kwan P, Brodie MJ. (2001). Neuropsychological effects of epilepsy and antiepileptic drugs. *Lancet*, 357: 216-222.

Lauterborn JC, Ribak CE. (1989). Differences in dopamine beta-hydroxylase immunoreactivity between the brains of genetically epilepsy-prone and Sprague-Dawley rats. *Epilepsy Res.*, 4: 161-176.

Laurberg, S., and J. Zimmer. (1981). Lesion-induced sprouting of hippocampal mossy fiber collaterals to the fascia dentata in developing and adult rats. *J. Comp. Neurol.*, 200: 433-459.

Law-Tho D, Hirsch JC, Crepel F. (1994). Dopamine modulation of synaptic transmission in rat prefrontal cortex: an in vitro electrophysiological study. *Neurosci. Res.*, 21: 151-160.

Lazarova M, Bendotti C, Samanin R. (1983). Studies on the role of serotonin in different regions of the rat central nervous system on pentylenetetrazol-induced seizures and the effect of Di-n-propyl-acetate. *Arch. Pharmacol.*, 322: 147-152.

Le Poul E, Boni C, Hanoun N, Laporte AM, Laaris N, Chauveau J, Hamon M, Lanfumey L. (2000). Differential adaptation of brain 5-HT1A and 5-HT1B receptors and 5-HT transporter in rats treated chronically with fluoxetine. *Neuropharmacology*, 39: 110-122.

Lennox WG. (1942). Brain injury, drugs, and environment as causes of mental decay in epilepsy. *Am. J. Psychiatry.*, 99: 174-180.

Lewis BL, O'Donnell P. (2000).Ventral tegmental area afferents to the prefrontal cortex maintain membrane potential 'up' states in pyramidal neurons via D(1) dopamine receptors. *Cereb. Cortex*, 10: 1168-1175.

Lewis PA, Miall RC. (2003). Distinct systems for automatic and cognitively controlled time measurement: Evidence from neuroimaging. *Curr. Opin. Neurobiol.*, 13: 250-255.

Lewis PR, Shute CCD. (1967). The cholinergic limbic system: projections to hippocampal formation, medial cortex, nuclei of the ascending cholinergic reticular system, and the subfornical organ and supra-optic crest. *Brain.*, 90: 521-540.

Lidov HGW, Grzanna R, Molliver ME. (1980). The serotonin innervation of the cerebral cortex in the rat - an immunohistochemical analysis. *Neuroscience*, 5: 207-227.

Lisman JE, Fellous, Jean-Marc, Wang, Xiao-Jing. (1998). A role for NMDA-receptor channels in working memory. *Nature Neuroscience*, 1: 273-275.

Litt B, Esteller R, Echauz J, D'Alessandro M, Shor R, Henry T, Pennell P, Epstein C, Bakay R, Dichter M, Vachtsevanos G. (2001). Epileptic seizures may begin hours in advance of clinical onset: a report of five patients. *Neuron*, 30: 51-64.

Liu Z, Nagao T, Desjardins QC, Gloor P, Avoli M. (1994). Quantitative evaluation of neuronal loss in the dorsal hippocampus in rats with long-term pilocarpine seizures. *Epilepsy Res.*, 17: 237-247.

Lopez-Bayghen E, Espinoza-Rojo M, Ortega A. (2003). Glutamate down-regulates GLAST expression through AMPA receptors in Bergmann glial cells. *Mol. Br. Res.*, 115: 1-9.

Lopes da Silva FH, Witter MP, Boeijinga PH, Lohman HM. (1990). Anatomic organization and physiology of the limbic cortex. *Physiol. Rev.*, 76: 453-511.

Loscher W, Czuczwar SJ. (1987). Comparison of drugs with different selectivity for central alpha1 and alpha2-adrenoceptors in animal models of epilepsy. *Epilepsy Res.*, 1: 165-172.

Loscher W, Schmidt D. (1988). Which animal models should be used in the search for new antiepileptic drugs? A proposal based on experimental and clinical considerations. *Epilepsy Res.,* 2: 145-181.

Loscher WC. (2002). Current status and future directions in the pharmacotherapy of epilepsy. *Trends. Pharmacol. Sci.,* 23: 113-118.

Lothman EW, Bertram EH, Stringer JL. (1991). Functional anatomy of hippocampal seizures. *Prog. Neurobiol.,* 37: 1-82.

Lowry OH, Roserbrough NJ, Farr AL, Randall RJ. (1951). Protein measurements and folin phenol reagent. *J. Biol. Chem.,* 193: 265-275.

Lubbert H, Hoffman BJ, Snutch TP, van Dyke T, Levine AJ, Hartig PR, Lester HA, Davidson N. (1987). cDNA cloning of a serotonin 5-HT$_{1C}$ receptor by electrophysiological assays of mRNA-injected Xenopus oocytes. *Proc. Natl. Acad. Sci. USA*, 84: 4332-4336.

Lysakowski A, Wainer BH, Bruce G, Hersh LB. (1989). An atlas of the regional and laminar distribution of choline acetyltransferase immunoreactivity in rat cerebral cortex. *Neuroscience*, 28: 291-336.

MacDermott AB, Mayer ML, Westbrook GL, Smith SJ, Barker JL. (1986). NMDA-receptor activation increases cytoplasmic calcium concentration in cultured spinal cord neurones. *Nature*, 321: 519-522.

Mahanty NK, Sah P. (1999). Excitatory synaptic inputs to pyramidal neurons of the lateral amygdala. *Eur. J. Neurosci.,* 11: 1217-1222.

Malhotra CL, Das PK. (1959). Pharmacological studies of *Herpestis monniera Linn.* (Brahmi). *Indian J. Med. Res.,* 47: 294-305.

Manford M, Hart YM, Sander JW, Shorvon SD. (1992). National General Practice Study of Epilepsy (NGPSE): partial seizure patterns in a general population. *Neurology*, 42: 1911-1917.

Marco P, DeFelipe J. (1997). Altered synaptic circuitary in human temporal neocortex remove from epileptic patients. *Exp. Brain Res.*, 114: 1-10.

Maricq AV, Peterson AS, Brake AJ, Myers RM, Julius D. (1991). Primary structure and functional expression of the 5HT$_3$ receptor, a serotonin-gated ion channel. *Science*, 254: 432-437.

Martin C, Martin S, Viret R, Denis J, Mirguet F, Diserbo M, Multon E, Lamproglou I. (2001). Low dose of the gamma acute radiation syndrome does not significantly alter either cognitive behavior or dopaminergic and serotoninergic metabolism. *Cell Mol.Biol.*, 47: 459-65.

Martis G, Rao A. (1992). Neuropharmacological Activity of *Herpestis monniera. Fitoterapia*, 63: 399-404.

Marvel CL, Schwartz BL, Rosse RB. (2004). A quantitative measure of postural sway deficits in schizophrenia. *Schizophr. Res.*, 68: 363-372.

Mason ST, Corcoran ME. (1979). Catecholamines and convulsions. *Brain Res.*, 170: 497-507.

Matsuoka H, Ishii M, Sugimoto T, Hirata Y, Sugimoto T, Kangawa K, Matsuo H. (1985). Inhibition of aldosterone production by alpha-human atrial natriuretic polypeptide is associated with an increase in cGMP production. *Biochem. Biophys.Res.Commun.*, 127: 1052-1056.

Maura G, Marcoli M, Pepicelli O, Rosu C, Viola C, Raiteri M. (2000). Serotonin inhibition of the NMDA receptor/nitric oxide/cyclic GMP pathway in human neocortex slices: involvement of 5-HT$_{2C}$ and 5-HT$_{1A}$ receptors. *Br. J. Pharmacol.*, 130: 1853-1938.

Mazarati AM, Hal'aszi E, Telegdy G. (1992). Anticonvulsive effects of galanin administered into the central nervous system upon the picrotoxin-kindled seizure syndrome in rats. *Brain Res.*, 589: 164-166.

Mazarati AM, Liu H, Soomets U, Sankar R, Shin D, Katsumori H, Langel U, Wasterlain CG. (1998). Galanin modulation of seizures and seizure modulation of hippocampal galanin in animal models of status epilepticus. *J. Neurosci.*, 18: 10070-10077.

Mazarati Andréy, Siddarth Prabha, Baldwin Roger A, Shin Don, Caplan Rochelle, Sankar Raman. (2008). Depression after status epilepticus: behavioural and biochemical deficits and effects of fluoxetine. Brain, 131: 2071-2083.

McBean GJ, Roberts PJ. (1985). Neurotoxicity of L-glutamate and DL-thre-3-hydroxyaspartate in the rat striatum. *J. Neurochem.*, 44: 247-254.

McCormick DA, Contreras D. (2001). On the cellular and network bases of epileptic seizures. *Annu. Rev. Physiol.,* 63: 815-846.

McCormick DA, Pape H-C. (1990). Noradrenergic and serotonergic modulation of a hyperpolarization-activated cation current in thalamic relay neurones. *J. Physiol.,* 431: 319-342.

McCormick DA, Wang Z, Huguenard JR. (1993). Neurotransmitter control of neocortical neuronal activity and excitability. *Cereb. Cortex,* 3: 387-398.

McDonald J, Garofala E, Hood T. (1991). Altered excitatory and inhibitory amino acid receptor binding in hippocampus of patients with temporal lobe epilepsy. *Ann. Neurol.*, 29: 529-541.

McGeer PL, Eccles JC, McGeer EG. (1987). Putative excitatory neurons: Glutamate and aspartate. *In, Molecular Neurobiology of the Mammalian Brain*, McGeer PL, Eccles JC, and McGeer EG (Eds.). New York: Plenum Press, 175-196.

McKinney RA, Debanne D, Gähwiler BH, Thompson SM (1997) Lesion-induced axonal sprouting and hyperexcitability in the hippocampus in vitro: implications for the genesis of posttraumatic epilepsy. Nat. Med., 3: 990-996.

Mechiel Korte S, De Boer SF. (2003). A robust animal model of state anxiety: fear-potentiated behaviour in the elevated plus-maze. *Eur. J. Phamacol.*, 463: 163-175.

Meldrum BS, Bruton CJ. (1992). Epilepsy. In:Greenfield's Neuropathology (Adams JH, Duchen LW eds), New York: Oxford University Press. 1246-1238.

Mellgren SI, Srebro B. (1973). Changes in acetylcholinesterase and distribution of degenerating fibres in the hippocampal region after septal lesions in the rat. *Brain Res.*, 52: 19-36.

Mello LE, Cavalheiro EA, Tan AM, Kupfer WR, Pretorius JK, Babb TL, Finch DM. (1993). Circuit mechanisms of seizures in the pilocarpine model of chronic epilepsy: cell loss and mossy fiber sprouting. *Epilepsia,* 34: 985- 995.

Meltzer CC, Smith G, DeKosky ST, Pollock BG, Mathis CA, Moore RY, Kupfer DJ, Reynolds CF. (1998). Serotonin in Aging, Late-Life Depression, and Alzheimer's Disease: The Emerging Role of Functional Imaging. *Neuropsychopharmacology,* 18: 407-430.

Menard J, Treit D. (1999). Effects of centrally administered anxiolytic compounds in animal models of anxiety. *Neurosci. Biobehav. Rev.,* 23: 591-613.

Millan MJ, Dekeyne A, Papp M, Drieu La Rochelle C, Macsweeny C, Peglion JL, Brocco M. (2001). S33005, a novel ligand at both serotonin and norepinephrine transporters: II. Behavioral profile in comparison with venlafaxine, reboxetine, citalopram and clomipramine. *J.Phar.Exp.Ther.,* 298: 581-591.

Millan MJ, Gobert A, Lejeune F, Dekeyne A, Newman-Tancredi A, Pasteau V, Rivet JM, Cussac D. (2003). The novel melatonin agonist agomelatine (S20098) is an antagonist at 5-HT2C receptors, blockade of which enhances the activity of frontocortical dopaminergic and adrenergic pathways. *J. Pharmacol. Exp. Ther.,* 306: 954-964.

Millan MJ. (2005). 5-HT$_{2C}$ receptors as a target for the treatment of depressive and anxious states: focus on novel therapeutic strategies. *Therapie,* 60: 441-460.

Millan MJ. (2006). Multi-target strategies for the improved treatment of depressive states: conceptual foundations and neuronal substrates, drug discovery and therapeutic application. *Pharmacol. Ther.,* 110: 135-370.

Milner TA, Loy R, Amaral DG. (1983). An anatomical study of the development of the septo-hippocampal projection in the rat. *Dev. Brain. Res.,* 8: 343-371.

Mishra PK, Burger RL, Bettendorf AF, Browning RA, Jobe PC. (1994). Role of norepinephrine in forebrain and brainstem seizures: chemical lesioning of locus ceruleus with DSP4. *Exp. Neurol.,* 125: 58-64.

Mitchell SJ, Ranck JBJ. (1980). Generation of theta rhythm in medial entorhinal cortex of freely moving rats. *Brain Res.,* 189: 49-66.

Mitsuyoshi I, Ito M, Shirasaka Y, Mikawa H, Serikawa T, Yamada J. (1993). Changes of NMDA receptor binding in spontaneously epileptic rat and parent strains. *Neurochem. Res.*, 18: 1169-1173.

Moldrich RX, Chapman AG, De Sarro G, Meldrum BS. (2003). Glutamate metabotropic receptors as targets for drug therapy in epilepsy. *Eur. J. Pharmacol.*, 476: 3-16.

Monkawa T, Miyawaki A, Sugiyama T, Yoneshima H, Yamamoto-Hino M, Furuichi T, Saruta T, Hasegawa M, Mikoshiba K. (1995). Heterotetrameric complex formation of inositol 1,4,5-trisphosphate receptor subunits. *J.Biol.Chem.*, 270: 14700-14704.

Moore RY, Halaris AE. (1975). Hippocampal innervation by serotonin neurons of the midbrain raphe in the rat. *J.Comp.Neurol.*, 164: 171-183.

Morita T, Tanimura A, Nexu A, Tojyo Y. (2002). Visualization of inositol 1,4,5-trisphosphate receptor type III with green fluorescent protein in living cells. *Cell Calcium*, 31: 59-64.

Morita T, Tanimura A, Nezu A, Kurosaki T, Tojyo Y. (2004). Functional analysis of the green fluorescent protein-tagged inositol 1,4,5-trisphosphate receptor type 3 in Ca2+ release and entry in DT40 B lymphocytes. *Biochem.J.*, 382: 793-801.

Morris RGM, Schenk F, Tweedie F, Jarrard LE. (1990). Ibotenate lesions of hippocampus and subiculumP: dissociating components of allocentric spatial learning. *Eur. J. Neurosci.*, 2: 1016-1028.

Movsesyan VA, O'Leary DM, Fan L, Bao W, Mullins PG, Knoblach SM, Faden AI. (2001). mGluR5 antagonists 2-methyl-6-(phenylethynyl)- pyridine and (E)-2-methyl-6-(2-phenylethenyl)-pyridine reduce traumatic neuronal injury *in vitro* and *in vivo* by antagonizing N-methyl-D-aspartate receptors. *J. Pharmacol. Exp. Ther.*, 296: 41-47.

Muller M, Gahwiler BH, Rietschin L, Thompson SM. (1993). Reversible loss of dendritic spines and altered excitability after chronic epilepsy in hippocampal slice cultures. *Proc. Natl. Acad. Sci. USA.*, 90: 257-261.

Multani P, Myers RH, Blume HW, Schomer DL, Sotrel A. (1994). Neocortical dendritic pathology in human partial epilepsy: a quantitative Golgi study. *Epilepsia*, 35: 718-736.

Murphy SN, Miller RJ. (1988). A glutamate receptor regulates Ca2+ mobilization in hippocampal neurons. *Proc. Natl. Acad. Sci. USA*, 85: 8737-8741.

Murray TF, Sylvester D, Schultz CS, Szot P. (1985). Purinergic modulation of pentylenetetrazol seizure threshold in the rat. *Neuropharmacology*, 24: 761-766.

Nagao T, Alonso A, Avoli M. (1996). Epileptiform activity induced by pilocarpine in combined slice of the rat hippocampus-entorhinal cortex. *Neuroscience,* 72: 399-408.

Nagarkatti N, Deshpande LS, DeLorenzo RJ. (2008). Levetiracetam inhibits both ryanodine and IP3 receptor activated calcium induced calcium release in hippocampal neurons in culture. *Neurosci Lett.* 436:289-93.

Nakayama T, Kawakami H, Tanaka K, Nakamura S. (1996). Expression of three glutamate transporter subtype mRNAs in human brain regions and peripheral tissues. *Mol. Brain Res.*, 36: 189-192.

Neumeister A, Konstantinidis A, Stastny J, Schwarz MJ, Vitouch O, Willeit M, Praschak-Rieder N, Zach J, de Zwann M, Bondy B, Ackenheil M, Kasper S. (2002). Association between serotonin transporter gene promoter polymorphism (5HTTLPR) and behavioral responses to tryptophan depletion in healthy women with and without family history of depression. *Arch. Gen. Psychiatry*, 59: 613-620.

Nicholls D, Attwell D. (1990). The release and uptake of excitatory amino acids. *Trends Pharmacol. Sci.*, 11: 462-468.

Niswender CM, Copeland SC, Herrick-Davis K, Emerson RB, Saunders-Bush E. (1999). RNA editing of the human serotonin 5- hydroxytryptamine 2C receptor silences constitutive activity. *J. Biol. Chem.*, 274: 9472-9478.

O'Leary DM, Movsesyan V, Vicini S, Faden AI. (2000). Selective mGluR5 antagonists MPEP and SIB-1893 decrease NMDA or glutamate-mediated neuronal toxicity through actions that reflect NMDA receptor antagonism. *Br. J. Pharmacol.*, 131: 1429-1437.

O'Dell LE, Kreifeldt MJ, George FR, Ritz MC. (2000). The role of serotonin (2) receptors in mediating cocaine-induced convulsions. *Pharmacol. Biochem. Behav.*, 65: 677-681.

Oh S, Hoshi K, Ho IK. (1997). Role of NMDA receptors in pentobarbital tolerance/dependence. *Neurochem. Res.*, 22: 767-774.

Olivier JDA, Hart Van Der, Swelm Van RPL, Dederen PJ, Homberg JR, Cremers T, Deen PMT, Cuppen A, Cools AR, Ellenbroek BA. (2008). Neuroscience, 152: 573-584.

Olney J, Farber N. (1995). Glutamate receptor dysfunction and schizophrenia. *Arch. Gen. Psychiatry*, 52: 998-1007.

Olney J W, Price MT, Fuller T A, Labruyere J, Samson L, Carpenter M, Mahan K (1986). The anti-excitotoxic effects of certain anaesthetics, analgesics and sedative- hypnotics. Neurosci. Lett. 68: 29-34.

Olney JW. (1989). Excitotoxicity and N-methyl-D-aspartate receptors. *Drug Dev. Res.*, 17: 299-319.

Ortells MO, Lunt GG. (1995). Evolutionary history of the ligand-gated ion-channel superfamily of receptors. *Trends Neurosci.*, 18: 121-127.

Otoya RE, Seltzer AM, Donoso AO. (1997). Acute and long lasting effects of neonatal hypoxia on (+)-3-[^{135}I] MK-801 binding to NMDA brain receptors. *Experimental Neurology*, 148: 92-99.

Ottersen OP, Storm-mathisen J. (1984). Neurons containing or accumulating transmitter amino acids. *In Handbook of Chemical Neuroanatomy. Vol. 3: Classical Transmitters and Transmitter Receptors in the CNS, Part II. ed.* Amsterdam, New York, Oxford: Elsevier Science Publishers B.V, :191-198.

Oulad Ben Taib N, Manto M. (2006). Hemicerebellectomy impairs the modulation of cutaneomuscular reflexes by the motor cortex following repetitive somatosensory stimulation. *Brain Res.*, 1090: 110-115.

Overbeck B, Grunwald F, Reinke U, Bockisch A, Gratz KF, Biersack HJ. (1990). Early and late HMPAO-SPECT during an epileptic seizure. *Nuklearmedizin*, 29: 228-230.

Pal R, Dwivedi AK, Singh S, Kulshrestha DK. (1998). High performance liquid chromatographic (HPLC) quantification of bacosides in *Bacopa monnieri* extracts. *Indian J. Pharm.Sci.*, 60: 328-329.

Pal R, Sarin JPS. (1992). Quantitative determination of bacosides by UV spectrophotometry. *Indian J. Pharm. Sci.*, 54: 17-18.

Palacios J, Waeber C, Hoyer D, Mengod G. (1990). Distribution of serotonin receptors. *Ann. NY Acad. Sci.*, 600: 36-52.

Parent JM, Yu TW, Leibowitz RT, Geschwind DH, Sloviter RS, Lowenstein DH. (1997). Dentate granule cell neurogenesis is increased by seizures and contributes to aberrant network reorganization in the adult hippocampus. *J. Neurosci.*, 17: 3727-3738.

Park CH, Kim SM, Streletz LJ, Zhang J, Intenzo C. (1992). Reverse crossed cerebellar diaschisis in partial complex seizures related to herpes simplex encephalitis. *Clin. Nucl. Med.*, 17: 732-735.

Pasini A, Tortorella A, Gale K. (1996). The anticonvulsant action of fluoxentine in subsatntia nigra is dependent upon endogeneous serotonin. *Brain Res.*, 724: 84-88.

Patel S, Roberts J, Moorman J, Reavill C. (1995). Localization of serotonin-4 receptors in the striatonigral pathway in rat brain. *Neuroscience*, 69: 1159-1167.

Paulose CS, Dakshinamurthi K, Packer S, Stephens NL. (1988). Sympathetic stimulation and hypertension in pyridoxine deficient adult rats. *Hypertension*, 11: 387-391.

Paulose CS, Finla C, Reas KS, Amee K. (2008). Neuroprotective role of *Bacopa monnieri* extract in epilepsy and effect of glucose supplementation during hypoxia: glutamate receptor gene expression. *Neurochem. Res.*, 33: 1663-1671.

Pazos A, Hoyer D, Palacios JM. (1984). The binding of serotonergic ligands to the porcine choroid plexus, characterization of a new type of serotonin recognition site. *Eur. J. Pharmacol.*, 106: 539-546.

Pelligrino DA, Wang Q. (1998). Cyclic nucleotide crosstalk and the regulation of cerebral vasodilation. *Prog.Neurobiol.*, 56: 1-18.

Pellow S, Chopin P, Files SE, Briley M. (1985). Validation of open: Closed arm entries in an elevated plus-maze as a measure of anxiety in the rat. *J.Neurosc. Meth.*, 14: 149-167.

Penit-Soria J, Audinat E, Crepel F. (1987). Excitation of rat prefrontal cortical neurons by dopamine: an in vitro electrophysiological study. *Brain Res.*, 425: 263-274.

Perez Y, Morin F, Beaulieu C, Lacaille JC. (1996). Axonal sprouting of CA1 pyramidal cells in hyperexcitable hippocampal slices of kainate-treated rats. *Eur. J. Neurosci.*, 8: 736-748.

Peroutka SJ. (1994). Molecular biology of serotonin (5-HT) receptors. *Synapse*, 18: 241-260.

Pin JP, Duvoisin R. (1995). Reveiw: Neurotransmitter receptors I. The Metabotropic glutamate receptors: structure and functions. *Neuropharmacology*, 34: 1-26.

Pines G, Danbolt NC, Bjoras M, Zhang Y, Bendahan A, Eide L, Koepsell H, Storm-Mathisen J, Seeberg JS, Kanner BI. (1992). Cloning and expression of a rat L-glutamate transporter. *Nature*, 360: 464-467.

Pintor M, Mefford IN, Hutter I, Pocotte SL, Wyler AR, Nadi NS. (1990). The levels of biogenic amines, their metabolites and tyrosine hydroxylase in the human epileptic temporal cortex. *Synapse*, 5: 152-156.

Pirot S, Godbout R, Mantz J, Tassin J-P, Glowinski J, Thierry AM. (1992). Inhibitory effects of ventral tegmental area stimulation on the activity of prefrontal cortical neurons: evidence for the involvement of both dopaminergic and GABAergic components. *Neuroscience*, 49: 857-865.

Ploghause A, Tracey I, Gati JS, Clare S, Menon RS, Matthews PM, Rawlins JNP. (1999). Dissociating pain from its anticipation in the human brain. *Science*, 284: 1979-1981.

Porsolt RD, Le Pichon M, Jalfre M. (1977). Depression: a new animal model sensitive to antidepressant treatments. *Nature*, 266: 730-732.

Prakash JC, Sirsi M. (1962). Comparative study of the effects of Brahmi (*Bacopa monniera*) and Chlopromazine on motor learning in rats. *J. Sci. Ind. Res.*, 21: 93-96.

Prakash O, Singh GN, Singh RM, Mathur SC, Bajpai M, Yadav S. (2008). Determination of bacoside A by HPTLC in *Bacopa monnieri* extract. *International Journal of Green Pharmacy*, 2: 173-175.

Price RD, Sanders-Bush E. (2000). RNA editing of the human serotonin 5-HT$_{2C}$ receptor delays agonist-stimulated calcium release. *Mol. Pharmacol.*, 58: 859-862.

Pyroja S, Binoy J, Paulose CS. (2007). Increased 5-HT$_{2c}$ receptor binding in the brain stem and cerebral cortex during liver regeneration and hepatic neoplasia in rats. *J. Neurol. Sci.*, 254: 3-8.

Quet F, Odermatt P, Preux Pierre-M. (2008). Challenges of epidemiological research on epilepsy in resource poor countries. *Neuroepidemiology*, 30: 3-5.

Rachel EB, Kevin DB, Victoria NL. (2003). Chronic stress effects on memory: sex differences in performance and monoaminergic activity. *Hormone and Behaviour*, 43: 48-59.

Racine RJ. (1972). Modification of seizure activity by electrical stimulation. I. After discharge threshold. *Electroencephalogr. Clin. Neurophysiol.*, 32: 269-279.

Rai D, Bhatia G, Palit G, Pal R, Singh S, Singh HK. (2003b). Adaptogenic effect of *Bacopa monniera* (Brahmi). *Pharmcology Biochemistry Behaviour*, 75: 823-830.

Rainnie DG, Asprodini EK, Shinnick-Gallagher P. (1991). Excitatory transmission in the basolateral amygdala. *J. Neurophysiol.*, 66: 986-998.

Rao SM, Harrington DL, Haaland KY, Bobholz JA, Cox RW, Binder JR. (1997). Distributed neural systems underlying the timing of movements. *J. Neurosci.*, 17: 5528-5535.

Rapport MM, Green AA, Page IH. (1948). Serum vasoconstrictor (serotonin) IV. *J. Biol. Chem.*, 176: 1243-1251.

Reader TA, Ferron A, Descarries L, Jasper HH. (1979). Modulatory role for biogenic amines in the cerebral cortex. Microiontophoretic studies. *Brain Res.*, 160: 217-229.

Reas SK, Amee K, Paulose CS. (2008). Glutamate receptor gene expression and binding studies in pilocarpine induced epileptic rat: neuroprotective role of *Bacopa monnieri* extract. *Epilep. Behav.*, 12: 54-60.

Reep RL, Corwin JV, Hashimoto A, Watson RT. (1987). Efferent connections of the rostral portion of medial agranular cortex in rats. *Brain Res. Bull.*, 19: 203-221.

Rege NN, Thatte UM, Dahanukar SA. (1999). Adaptogenic properties of six rasayanas herbs used in ayurvedic medicine. *Phytotherapy Research*, 13: 275-291.

Rice A, Rafiq A, Shapiro SM, Jakoi ER, Coulter DA, DeLorenzo RJ. (1996). Longlasting reduction of inhibitory function and GABA, receptor subunit mRNA expression in a model of temporal lobe epilepsy. *Proc. Natl. Acad. Sci. USA.*, 93: 9665-9669.

Richter-Levin G, Segal M. (1990). Effects of serotonin releasers on the dentate granular cell excitability in the rat. *Exp. Brain Res.*, 82: 199-207.

Robinson MB, Sinor JD, Dowd A, Kerwin JF. (1993). Subtypes of sodiumdependent high-affinity L-[3H] glutamate transport activity: Pharmacologic specificity and regulation by sodium and potassium. *J. Neurochem.*, 60: 167-179.

Roch C, Leroy C, Nehlig A Namer IJ. (2002). Predictive value of cortical injury for the development of temporal lobe epilepsy in 21- day-old rats: an MRI approach using the lithium-pilocarpine model. *Epilepsia*, 43: 1129-1136.

Rodgers RJ. (1997). Animal models of 'anxiety': where next? *Behav. Pharmacol.*, 8: 477-504.

Rogan MT, Stäubli UV, LeDoux JE. (1997). AMPA receptor facilitation accelerates fear learning without altering the level of conditioned fear acquired. *J. Neurosci.*, 17: 5928-5935.

Rohini G, Sabitha KE, Devi CS. (2004). *Bacopa monniera* Linn. Extract modulates antioxidant and marker enzyme status in fibrosarcoma bearing rats. *Indian J. Exp. Biol.*, 42: 776-780.

Romano C, Sesma MA, McDonald CT, O'Malley K, Van den Pol AN, Olney JW. (1995). Distribution of metabotropic glutamate receptor mGluR5 immunoreactivity in rat brain. *J. Comp. Neurol.*, 335: 455-469.

Room P, Groenewegen HJ. (1986). The connections of the parahippocampal cortex in the cat. I. Cortical afferents. *J. Comp. Neurol.*, 251: 415-450.

Rosane BB, Helena MTB. (2004). Carbamazepine enhances discriminative memory in rat model of epilepsy. *Epilepsia*, 45: 1443-1447.

Rosenmund C, Feltz A, Westbrook GL. (1995). Calcium-dependent inactivation of synaptic NMDA receptors in hippocampal neurons. *J. Neurophysiol.*, 73: 427-430.

Rothman SM, Olney JW. (1986). Glutamate and the pathophysiology of hypoxic-ischemic brain damage. *Ann Neurol.*, 19: 105-111.

Rothstein JD, Dykes-Hoberg M, Pardo CA, Bristol LA, Jin L, Kuncl RW, Kanai Y, Hediger MA, Wang Y, Schielke JP, Welty DF. (1996). Knockout of glutamate transporters reveals a major role for astroglial transport in excitotoxicity and clearance of glutamate. *Neuron*, 16: 675-686.

Rothstein JD, Martin L, Levey AI, Dykes-Hoberg M, Jin L, Wu D, Nash N, Kuncl RW. (1994). Localization of neuronal and glial glutamate transporters. *Neuron*, 13: 713-725.

Rothstein JD, Martin LJ, Kuncl RW. (1992). Decreased glutamate transport by the brain and spinal cord in amyotrophic lateral sclerosis. *N. Engl. J. Med.*, 326: 1464-1468.

Rothstein JD, Van Kammen M, Levey AI, Martin LJ, Kuncl RW. (1995). Selective loss of glial glutamate transporter GLT-1 in amyotrophic lateral sclerosis. *Ann. Neurol.*, 38: 78-84.

Royes LF, Fighera MR, Furian AF, Oliveira MS, Fiorenza NG, Petry JC, Coelho RC, Mello CF. (2007). The role of nitric oxide on the convulsive behavior and oxidative stress induced by methylmalonate: an electroencephalographic and neurochemical study. *Epilepsy Res.*, 73: 228-237.

Russo A, Borrelli F. (2005). *Bacopa monniera*, a reputed nootropic plant: an overview. *Phytomedicine*, 12: 305-317.

Russo A, Izzo AA, Borrelli F, Renis M, Vanella A. (2003). Free radical scavenging capacity and protective effect of *Bacopa monniera* L. on DNA damage. *Phytother. Res.*, 17: 870-875.

Sairam K, Dorababu M, Goel RK, Bhattacharya SK. (2002). Antidepressant activity of standardized extract of Bacopa monniera in experimental models of depression in rats. *Phytomedicine*, 9: 207-211.

Saltzman AG, Morse B, Whitman MM, Ivanshchenko Y, Jaye M, Felder S. (1991). Cloning of the human serotonin 5-HT$_2$ and 5-HT$_{1C}$ receptor subtypes. *Biochem. Biophys. Res. Comm.*, 181: 1469-1478.

Samad N, Haleem MA, Haleem DJ. (2008). Behavioral effects of 1-(m-chlorophenyl)piperazine (m-cpp) in a rat model of tardive dyskinesia. *Pak. J. Pharm. Sci.*, 21: 262-268.

Sander-Bush E, Fentress H, Hazelwood L. (2003). Serotonin 5-HT$_2$ receptors, molecular and genomic diversity. *Mol. Interv.*, 3: 319-330.

Sano H, Nagai Y, Miyakawa T, Shigemoto R, Yokoi M. (2008). Increased social interaction in mice deficient of the striatal medium spiny neuron-specific phosphodiesterase 10A2. *J. Neurochem.*, 105: 546-556.

Sardo P, Ferraro G. (2007). Modulatory effects of nitric oxide-active drugs on the anticonvulsant activity of lamotrigine in an experimental model of partial complex epilepsy in the rat. *BMC Neurosci.*, 8: 47.

Sarnyai Z, Sibille EL, Pavlides C, Fenster RJ, McEwen BS. (2000). T6th M. Impaired hippocampal-dependent learning and functional abnormalities in the hippocampus in mice lacking serotonin 1A receptors. *Proc. Natl. Acad. Sci. USA.*, 97: 14731-14736.

Saudou F, Hen R. (1994). 5-hydroxytryptamine receptor subtypes in vertebrates and invertebrates. *Neurochem. Int.*, 25: 503-532.

Savic I, Roland P, Sedvall F, Persson A, Pauli S, Widen L. (1988). *In vivo* demonstration of reduced benzodiazepine receptor binding in human epileptic foci. *Lancet*, 15: 863-866.

Scatchard G. (1949). The attraction of proteins for small molecules and ions. *Annals of the New York Academy of Sciences*, 51: 660-672.

Schiller Y. (2004). Activation of a calcium-activated cation current during epileptiform discharges and its possible role in sustaining seizure-like events in neocortical slices. *J. Neurophysiol.*, 92: 862-872.

Schlunzen, Saunders-Bush E, Burris KD, Knoth K. (1988). Lysergic acid diethylamide and 2,5-dimethoxy-4-methylamphetamine are partial agonists at serotonin receptors linked to phosphoinositide hydrolysis. *J. Pharmacol. Exp. Ther.*, 246: 924-928.

Schmahmann JD, Sherman JC. (1998). The cerebellar cognitive affective syndrome. *Brain*, 121: 561-579.

Schmidt-Kastner R, Ingvar M. (1996). Laminar damage of neurons and astrocytes in neocortex and hippocampus of rat after long-lasting status epilepticus induced by pilocarpine. *Epilepsy Res. Suppl.*, 12: 309-316.

Seamans JK, Durstewitz D, Christie BR, Stevens CF, Sejnowski TJ. (2001). Dopamine D1/D5 receptor modulation of excitatory synaptic inputs to layer V prefrontal cortex neurons. *Proc. Natl. Acad. Sci. USA.*, 98: 301-306.

Sesack SR, Bunney BS. (1989). Pharmacological characterization of the receptor mediating electrophysiological responses to dopamine in the rat medial prefrontal cortex: A microiontophoretic study. *J. Pharmacol. Exp. Ther.*, 249: 1323-1333.

Shankar PNE , Anu J, Paulose CS. (2007). Decreased [3H] YM-09151-2 binding to dopamine D2 receptors in the hypothalamus, brain stem and pancreatic islets of streptozotocin induced diabetic rats. *European J. Pharmacol.*, 557: 99-105.

Shanker G, Singh HK. (2000). Anxiolytic profile of standardized Brahmi extract. *Indian J. Pharmacol.*, 32: 152.

Shanmugasundaram ER, Akbar GK, Shanmugasundaram KR. (1991). Brahmighritham. An Ayurvedic herbal formula for the control of epilepsy. *J. Ethnopharmacol.*, 33: 269-276.

Sharp T, Bramwell DG, Grahame Smith. (1990). Release of endogenous 5-Hydroxy tryptamine in rat ventral hippocampus evoked by electrical stimulation of the dorsal raphe nucleus as detected by microdialysis; sensitivity to tetrodotoxin, calcium and calcium antagonists. *Neuroscience*, 39: 629-637.

Shashidharan P, Huntley GW, Murray JM, Buku A, Moran T, Walsh MJ, Morisson JH, Plaitakis A. (1997). Immunohistochemical localization of the neuron-specific glutamate transporter EAAC1 (EAAT3) in rat brain and spinal cord revealed by monoclonal antibody. *Brain Res.*, 773: 139-148.

Sheikh N, Ahmad A, Siripurapu KB, Kuchibhotla Vijaya K, Singh S, Palit G. (2007). Effect of *Bacopa monniera* on stress induced changes in plasma corticosterone and brain monoamines in rats. *Journal of Ethnopharmacology*, 111: 671-676.

Shen Y, Specht SM, De Saint Ghislain I, Li R. (1994). The hippocampus: a biological model for studying learning and memory. *Prog. Neurobiol.*, 44: 485-496.

Shrikumar S, Sandip S, Ravi TK, Umamaheswari M. (2004). Thin-layer chromatographic method for the estimation of bacoside A. *Indian J. Pharm. Sci.*, 66: 132-135.

Shu Y, Hasenstaub A, McCormick DA. (2003). Turning on and off recurrent balanced cortical activity. *Nature,* 423: 288-293.

Shuai JW, Jung P. (2003). Optimal ion channel clustering for intracellular calcium signaling. *Proc.Natl.Acad.Sci.USA*, 100: 506-510.

Singh HK, Dhawan BN. (1982). Effect of *Bacopa monniera* extract on avoidance responses in rat. *J. Ethnopharmacol.*, 5: 205-214.

Singh HK, Dhawan BN. (1992). Drugs affecting learning and memory. In: Tandon PN, Bijiani V, Wadhwa S. (Eds.), *Lectures in Neurobiology, Wiley Eastern, New Delhi*, 1: 189-207.

Singh HK, Dhawan BN. (1997). Neuropsychopharmacological effects of the Ayurvedic nootropic *Bacopa monnieri* Linn (Brahmi). *Indian J. Pharmacol.*, 29: S359-S365.

Singh HK, Rastogi RP, Srimal RC, Dhawan BN. (1988). Effect of bacosides A and B on avoidance responses in rats. *Phytother. Res.*, 2: 70-75.

Singh S, Eapen S, D'Souza SF. (2006). Cadmium accumulation and its influence on lipid peroxidation and antioxidative system in an aquatic plant, *Bacopa monnieri* L. *Chemosphere*, 62: 233-246.

Siniscalchi A, Calabresi P, Mercuri NB, Bernardi G. (1997). Epileptiform discharge induced by 4-aminopyridine in magnesium-free medium in neocortical neurons: physiological and pharmacological characterizations. *Neuroscience,* 81: 189-197.

Sloviter RS, Valiquette G, Abrams GM, Ronk EC, Sollas AL, Paul LA, Neurobort S. (1989). Selective loss of hippocampal granule cells in the mature rat brain after adrenalectomy. *Science.*243: 535-538.

Sloviter RS, Dean E, Sollas AL, Goodman JH. (1996). Apoptosis and necrosis induced in different hippocampal neuron populations by repetitive perforant path stimulation in the rat. *J. Comp. Neurol.*, 366: 516-533.

Sloviter RS (1987) Decreased hippocampal inhibition and a selective loss of interneurons in experimental epilepsy. *Science.* 235:73–76.

Sloviter RS, Nilaver G. (1987). Immunocytochemical localization of GABA-. cholecystokinin-vasoactive intestinal polypeptide and somatostatin-like immunoreactivity in the area dentata and hippocampus of the rat. *J. Comp. Neurol.*, 256: 42-60.

Sloviter RS. (1989). Calcium-binding protein (calbindin-D28k) and parvalbumin immunocytochemistry: localization in the rat hippocampus with specific reference to the selective vulnerability of hippocampal neurons to seizure activity. *J. Comp. Neurol.*, 280: 183-196.

Sloviter RS. (1991). Permanently altered hippocampal structure excitability and inhibition after experimental status epilepticus in the rat: the "dormant basket cell" hypothesis and its possible relevance to temporal lobe epilepsy. *Hippocampus*, 1: 41-66.

Sloviter RS. (1994). On the relationship between neuropathology and pathophysiology in the epileptic hippocampus of humans and experimental animals. *Hippocampus*, 4: 250-253.

Smolders I, Lindekens H, Clinckers R, Meurs A, O'Neill MJ, Lodge D, Ebinger G, Michotte Y. (2004). In vivo modulation of extracellular hippocampal glutamate and GABA levels and limbic seizures by group I and II metabotropic glutamate receptor ligands. *J. Neurochem.*, 88: 1068-1077.

Smolders I, Van Belle K, Ebinger G, Michotte Y. (1997). Hippocampal and cerebellar extracellular amino acids during pilocarpine-induced seizures in freely moving rats. *Eur. J. Pharmacol.*, 319: 21-29.

Smythies J. (2005). Serotonin system. Int. Rev. *Neurobiol.*, 64: 217-268.

Snead III OC. (1987). Noradrenergic mechanisms in gammahydroxybutyrate- induced seizure activity. *Eur. J. Pharmacol.*, 136: 103-108.

Spencer RM, Zelaznik HN, Diedrichsen J, Ivry RB. (2003). Disrupted timing of discontinuous but not continuous movements by cerebellar lesions. *Science*, 300: 1437-1439.

Spencer S. (2007). Epilepsy: clinical observations and novel mechanisms. *Lancet Neurol.*, 6: 14-16.

Spooren WP, Gasparini F, Bergmann R, Kuhn R. (2000). Effects of the prototypical mGlu(5) receptor antagonist 2-methyl-6-(phenylethynyl)- pyridine on rotarod, locomotor activity and rotational responses in unilateral 6-OHDA-lesioned rats. *Eur. J. Pharmacol.*, 406: 403-410.

Spooren WP, Gasparini F, Salt TE, Kuhn R. (2001). Novel allosteric antagonists shed light on mglu(5) receptors and CNS disorders. *Trends Pharmacol. Sci.*, 22: 331-337.

Stachowicz K, Chojnacka-Wojcik E, Klak K, Pilc A. (2006). Anxiolytic-like effects of group III mGlu receptor ligands in the hippocampus involve GABA(A) signaling. *Pharmacol. Rep.*, 58: 820-826.

Stanford MS, Helfritz LE, Conklin SM, Villemarette-Pittman NR, Greve KW, Adams D, Houston RJ. (2005). A comparison of anticonvulsants in the treatment of impulsive aggression. *Exp. Clin. Psychopharmacol.*, 13: 72-77.

Starr MS. (1996). The role of dopamine in epilepsy. *Synapse*, 22: 159-194.

Statnick MA, Dailey JW, Jobe PC, Browning RA. (1996). Abnormalities in brain serotonin concentration, high-affinity uptake, and tryptophan hydroxylase activity in severe-seizure genetically epilepsy-prone rats. *Epilepsia*, 37: 311-321.

Steffens M, Huppertz HJ, Zentner J, Chauzit E, Feuerstein TJ. (2005). Unchanged glutamine synthetase activity and increased NMDA receptor density in epileptic human neocortex: Implications for the pathophysiology of epilepsy. *Neurochemistry International*, 47: 379-384.

Steward O, Scoville SA. (1976). The cells of origin of entorhinal afferents to the hippocampus and fascia dentata of the rat. *J. Comp. Neurol.*, 169: 347-370.

Stief F, Zuschratter W, Hartmann K, Schmitz D, Draguhn A. (2007). Enhanced synaptic excitation-inhibition ratio in hippocampal interneurons of rats with temporal lobe epilepsy. *Eur. J. Neurosci.*, 25: 519-528.

Storck T, Schulte S, Hofmann K, Stoffel W. (1992). Structure, expression and functional analysis of a Na1-dependent glutamate/aspartate transporter from the rat brain. *Proc. Natl. Acad.Sci. USA*, 89: 10955-10959.

Strine TW, Kobau R, Chapman DP, Thurman DJ, Price P, Balluz LS. (2005). Psychological distress, comorbidities, and health behaviors among U.S. adults with seizures: results from the 2002 National Health Interview Survey. *Epilepsia*, 46: 1133-1139.

Sudha B, Paulose CS. (1998). Induction of DNA synthesis in primary cultures of rat hepatocytes by serotonin: possible involvement of Serotonin S2 receptors. *Hepatology*, 27: 62-66.

Sullivan HC, Osorio I. (1991). Aggravation of penicillin-induced epilepsy in rats with locus ceruleus lesion. *Epilepsia.*, 32: 591-596.

Suppes T, Kriegstein AR, Prince DA. (1985). The influence of dopamine on epileptiform burst activity in hippocampal pyramidal neurons. *Brain Res.,* 326: 273-280.

Sutherland EW. (1972). Studies on the mechanism of hormone action. *Science*, 177: 401-408.

Sutula T, Koch J, Golarai G, Watanabe Y, McNamara JO. (1996). NMDA receptor dependence of kindling and mossy fiber sprouting: evidence that the NMDA receptor regulates patterning of hippocampal circuits in the adult brain. *J. Neuroscience.*, 16: 7398-7406.

Suvarna NU, O'Donnell JM. (2002). Hydrolysis of N-methyl-D-aspartate receptor-stimulated cAMP and cGMP by PDE4 and PDE2 phosphodiesterases in primary neuronal cultures of rat cerebral cortex and hippocampus. *J.Pharmacol.Exp.Ther.*, 302: 249-256.

Swanson LW, Cowan WM. (1977). An autoradiographic study of the organization of the efferent connections of the hippocampal formation in the rat. *J. Comp. Neurol.*, 172: 49-84.

Swanson LW, Kohler C. (1986). Anatomical evidence for direct projections from the entorhinal area to the entire cortical mantle in the rat. *J. Neurosci.*, 6: 3010-3023.

Swillens S, Dupont G, Combettes L, Champeil P. (1999). From calcium blips to calcium puffs: Theoretical analysis of the requirements for interchannel communication. *Proc.Natl.Acad.Sci.USA*, 96: 13750-13755.

Szyndler J, Wierzba-Bobrowicz T, Skórzewska A, Maciejak P, Walkowiak J, Lechowicz W, Turzyńska D, Bidziński A, Płaźnik A. (2005). Behavioral, biochemical and histological studies in a model of pilocarpine-induced spontaneous recurrent seizures. *Pharmacol. Biochem. Behav.*, 81: 15-23.

Takase K, Shigeto H, Suzuki SO, Kikuchi H, Ohyagi Y, Kira J. (2008). Prenatal freeze lesioning produces epileptogenic focal cortical dysplasia. *Epilepsia*, 49: 997-1010.

Tallaksen-Greene SJ, Kaatz KW, Romano C, Albin RL. (1998). Localization of mGluR1a-like immunoreactivity and mGluR5- like immunoreactivity in identified populations of striatal neurons. *Brain Res.*, 780: 210-217.

Tanaka J, Ryoichi I, Watanabe M, Tanaka K, Inoue Y. (1997). Extra-junctional localization of glutamate transporter EAAT4 at excitatory Purkinje cell synapses. *Neuroreport*, 8: 2461-2464.

Tanaka K, Watase K, Manabe T, Yamada K, Watanabe M, Takahashi K, Iwama H, Nishikawa T, Ichihara N, Hori S, Takimoto M, Wada K. (1997). Epilepsy and xacerbation of brain injury in mice lacking the glutamate transporter GLT1. *Science*, 276: 1699-1702.

Tateishi Y, Hattori M, Nakayama T, Iwai M, Bannai H, Nakamura T, Michikawa T, Inoue T, Mikoshiba K. (2005). Cluster formation of inositol 1, 4, 5-trisphosphate receptor requires its transition to open state. *J. Biol. Chem.*, 280: 6816-6822.

Tauck DL, Nadler JV. (1985). Evidence of functional mossy fiber sprouting in hippocampal formation of kainic acid-treated rats. *J. Neurosci.*, 5: 1016-1022.

Taylor CW, Genazzani AA, Morris SA. (1999). Expression of inositol trisphosphate receptors. *Cell Calcium*, 26: 237-251.

Tecott LH, Logue SF, Wehner JM, Kauer JA. (1998). Perturbed dentate gyrus function in serotonin 5-HT$_{2C}$ receptor mutant mice. *Proc. Natl. Acad. Sci. USA*, 95: 15026-15031.

Tecott LH, Sun LM, Akana SF, Strack AM, Lowenstein DH, Dallman MF, Julius D. (1995). Eating disorder and epilepsy in mice lacking 5HT$_{2C}$ serotonin receptors. *Nature*, 374: 542-546.

Tetz LM, Rezk PE, Ratcliffe RH, Gordon RK, Steele KE, Nambiar MP. (2006). Development of a rat pilocarpine model of seizure status epilepticus that mimics chemical warfare nerve agent exposure. *Toxicol. Ind. Health.,* 22: 255-266.

Thierry AM, Mantz J, Glowinski J. (1992). Influence of dopaminergic and noradrenergic afferents on their target cells in the rat medial prefrontal cortex. *In: Frontal Lobe Seizures and Epilepsies*, Ed. Chauvel P, Delgado-Escueta AV, Halgren E, and Bancaud J. New York: Raven Press, 545-554.

Thompson SE, Ayman G, Woodhall GL, Jones RS. (2007). Depression of Glutamate and GABA Release by Presynaptic GABA(B) Receptors in the Entorhinal Cortex in Normal and Chronically Epileptic Rats. *Neurosignals*, 15: 202-215.

Thomas D, Lipp P, Berridge MJ, Bootman MD. (1998). Hormone-evoked elementary Ca2+ signals are not stereotypic, but reflect activation of different size channel clusters and variable recruitment of channels within a cluster. *J Biol Chem.* 273: 27130-27136.

Tojyo Y, Morita T, Nezu A, Tanimura A. (2008). The clustering of inositol 1,4,5-trisphosphate (IP(3)) receptors is triggered by IP(3) binding and facilitated by depletion of the Ca(2+) store. *J.Pharmacol.Sci.,* 107: 138-150.

Tomei L, Cope FO. (1991). Apoptosis: the molecular basis of cell death. Series: Current communications in cell & molecular biology; Volume 3. Plainview. N.Y. Cold Spring Harbor Laboratory Press.

Tran PV, Bymaster FP, McNamara RK, Potter WZ. (2003). Dual monoamine modulation for improved treatment of major depressive disorder. *J. Clin. Psychopharmacol.,* 23: 78-86.

Trottier S, Evrard B, Vignal JP, Scarabin JM, Chauvel P. (1996). The serotonergic innervation of the cerebral cortex in man and its changes in focal cortical dysplasia. *Epilepsy Res.,* 25: 79-106.

Trottier S, Lindvall O, Chauvel P, Bjorklund A. (1988). Facilitation of focal cobalt induced epilepsy after lesions of the noradrenergic locus coeruleus system. *Brain Res.*, 454: 308-314.

Tseng KY, O'Donnell P. (2004). Dopamine-glutamate interactions controlling prefrontal cortical pyramidal cell excitability involve multiple signaling mechanisms. *J. Neurosci.*, 23: 5131-5139.

Tsujimura A, Matsuki M, Takao K, Yamanishi K, Miyakawa T, Hashimoto-Gotoh T. (2008). Mice lacking the kf-1 gene exhibit increased anxiety- but not despair-like behavior. *Front. Behav. Neurosci.*, doi:10.3389/neuro. 08.004.

Turski L, Ikonomidou C, Turski WA, Bortolotto ZA, Cavalheiro EA. (1989). Review: Cholinergic mechanisms and epileptogenesis. The seizures induced by pilocarpine: a novel experimental model of intractable epilepsy. *Synapse,* 3: 154-171.

Turski WA, Cavalheiro EA, Schwarz M, Czuczwar SI, Kleinrok Z. Turski. (1983). Limbic seizures produced by pilocarpine in rats: behavioural electroencephalographic and neuropathological study. *Behav. Brain Res.,* 9: 315-335.

Tutka, Klonowski P, Dzieciuch J, Kleinrok Z, Czuczwar SJ. (1996). NGnitro- L-arginine differentially affects glutamate- or kainate-induced seizures. *NeuroReport*, 7: 1605-1608.

Twarog BM, Page IH. (1953). Serotonin content of some mammalian tissues and urine and a method for its dertermination. *Am. J. Physiol.*, 175: 157-161.

Unnerstall Jr. (1990). Computer analysis of binding data. *Methods in neurotransmitter receptor analysis.* Ed. Yamura H, Nas, Kuhar M. Raven press : 247-255.

Urban NN, Gonzalez-Burgos G, Henze DA, Lewis DA, Barrionuevo G. (2002). Selective reduction by dopamine of excitatory synaptic inputs to pyramidal neurons in primate prefrontal cortex. *J. Physiol.,* 539: 707-712.

Ure J, Baudry M, Perassolo M. (2006). Metabotropic glutamate receptors and epilepsy. *J. Neurol. Sci.*, 247: 1-9.

Valenti O, Conn PJ, Marino MJ. (2002). Distinct physiological roles of the Gq-coupled metabotropic glutamate receptors Co-expressed in the same neuronal populations. *J. Cell. Physiol.*, 191: 125-137.

Van Donkelaar P, Lee RG. (1994). Interactions between the eye and hand motor systems: Disruptions due to cerebellar dysfunction. *J. Neurophysiol.*, 72: 1674-1685.

Van Hoesen GW, Pandya DN. (1975). Some connections of the entorhinal (area 28) and perirhinal (area 35) cortices of the rhesus monkey. I. Temporal lobe afferents. *Brain Res.*, 95: 1-24.

Van Hoesen GW. (1982). The parahippocampal gyrus: new observations regarding its cortical connections in the monkey. *Trends Neurosci.*, 5: 345-350.

Van Ness PC, Awad IA, Estes M, Nguyen Q, Olsen RW. (1995). Neurosteroid modulation of benzodiazepine binding to neocortical GABA, receptors in human focal epilepsy varies with pathology. *Soc. Neurosci. Abstr.*, 21: 1516.

Vanderwolf CH, Baker GB. (1986). Evidence that serotonin mediates non-cholinergic neocortical low voltage fast activity, noncholinergic hippocampal rhythmical slow activity and contributes to intelligent behavior. *Brain Research*, 374: 342-356.

Velaz-Faircloth M, McGraw TS, Alandro MS, Fremeau RTJ, Kilberg MS, Anderson KJ. (1996). Characterization and distribution of the neuronal glutamate transporter EAAC1 in rat brain. *Am. J. Physiol.*, 271: C67-C75.

Vinters HV, Armstrong DL, Babb TL, Daumas-Duport C, Robitaille Y, Bruton CJ, Farrel MA. (1993). The neuropathology of human symptomatic epilepsy. *In: Surgical treatment of the epilepsies*, Engel JJr (ed), 2nd ed. Raven Press, New York : 593-608.

Vohora SB, Khanna T, Athar M. (1997). Protective role of *Bacopa monniera* on morphine induced hepatotoxicity in rats. *Fitoterapia*,68: 361.

Wada Y, Nakamura M, Hasegawa H, Yamaguchi N. (1992). Intra-hippocampal injection of 8-hydroxy-2-(di-n-propylamino)tetralin (8-OH-DPAT) inhibits partial and generalized seizures induced by kindling stimulation in cats. *Neurosci. Lett.*, 159: 179-182.

Wada Y, Shiraishi J, Nakamura M, Koshino Y. (1997). Effects of 5-HT3 receptor agonist 1-(m-chlorophenyl)-biguanide in the rat kindling model of epilepsy. *Brain Res.*, 759: 313-316.

Walker M. (2007). Neuroprotection in epilepsy. *Epilepsia*, 8: 66-68.

Walsh DA, Perkins JP, Krebs EG. (1968). n adenosine 3',5'-monophosphate-dependant protein kinase from rabbit skeletal muscle. *J. Biol. Chem.*, 10: 3763-3765.

Wang J, O'Donnell P. (2001). D1 dopamine receptors potentiate NMDA-mediated excitability increases in layer V prefrontal cortical pyramidal neurons. *Cereb. Cortex*, 11: 452-462.

Wassmer E, Davies P, Whitehouse WP, Green SH. (2003). Clinical spectrum associated with cerebellar hypoplasia. *Pediatr. Neurol.*, 28: 347-351.

Weinberger DR. (1988). Schizophrenia and the frontal lobe. *Trends Neurosci.*, 11: 367-370.

Wenger GR, Stitzel RE, Craig CR. (1973). The role of biogenic amines in the reserpine-induced alteration of minimal electroshock seizure thresholds in the mouse. *Neuropharmacology*, 12: 693-703.

White TL, Youngentoba SL. The effect of NMDA-NR2B receptor subunit over-expression on olfactory memory task performance in the mouse. *Brain Res.* 1027: 1-7.

Williams GV, Goldman-Rakic PS. (1995). Modulation of memory fields by dopamine D1 receptors in prefrontal cortex. *Nature,* 376: 572-575.

Wilson BS, Pfeiffer JR, Smith AJ, Oliver JM, Oberdorf JA, Wojcikiewicz RJH. (1998). Calcium-dependent clustering of inositol 1,4,5-trisphosphate receptors. *Mol. Biol. Cell*, 9: 1465-1478.

Winder DW, Conn PJ. (1992). Activation of metabotropic glutamate receptors in the hippocampus increases cyclic AMP accumulation. *J.Neurochem.*, 59: 375-378.

Winkler J, Suhr ST, Gage FH, Thal LJ, Fisher LJ. (1995). Essential role of neocortical acetylcholine in spatial memory. *Nature,* 375: 484-487.

Winson J. (1980). Influence of raphe nuclei on neuronal transmission from perforant pathway through dentate gyrus. *J. Neurophysiol.*, 44: 937-950.

Wisden W, Parker EM, Mahle KDAG, Nowak HP, Yocca F, Seeburg P, Voigt MM. (1993). Cloning and characterization of the rat 5-HT5B receptor. Evidence that the 5-HT5B receptor couples to a G protein in mammalian cell membranes. *FEBS Let.*, 133: 25-31.

Witkin JM, Baez M, Yu J, Eilcr WJ 2nd. (2008). mGlu5 receptor deletion does not confer seizure protection to mice. *Life Sci.*, 83: 377-380.

Witter MP, Groenewegen HJ, Lopes da Silva FH, Lohman AHM. (1989). Functional organization of the extrinsic and intrinsic circuitry of the arahippocampal region. *Prog. Neurobiol.*, 33: 161-253.

Wojcikiewicz RJH. (1995). Type I, II, and III inositol 1,4,5-trisphosphate receptors are unequally susceptible to down-regulation and are expressed in markedly different proportions in different cell types. *J. Biol. Chem.*, 270: 11678-11683.

Wood PL, Rao TS, Iyengar S, Lanthorn T, Monahan J, Cordi A, Sun E, Vazquez M, Gray N, Contreras P. (1990). A review of the in vitro and in vivo neurochemical characterization of the NMDA/PCP/glycine/ion channel receptor macrocomplex. *Neurochem. Res.*, 15: 217-230.

World Health Organization. (2005). International Bureau for Epilepsy, International League Against Epilepsy: Atlas - Epilepsy care in the world. Geneva: World Health Organization, 2005.

Wyneken U, Marengo JJ, Villanueva S, Soto D, Sandoval R, Gundelfinger ED, Orrego F. (2003). Epilepsy-induced changes in signalling systems of human and rat postsynaptic densities. *Epilepsia*, 44: 243-246.

Yan QS, Dailey JW, Steenbergen JL, Jobe PC. (1998). Anticonvulsant effect of enhancement of noradrenergic transmission in the superior colliculcus in genitically epilepsy-prone rats (GEPRs): a microinjection study. *Brain Res.*, 780: 199-209.

Yan QS, Jobe PC, Dailey JW. (1995). Further evidence of anticonvulsant role of 5-hydroxytryptamine in genetically epilepsy-prone rats. *Br. J. Pharmacol.*, 115: 1314-1318.

Yan QS, Mishra PK, Burger RL, Bettendorf AF, Jobe PC, Dailey JW. (1992). Evidence that carbamazepine and antiepilepsirine may produce a component of their anticonvulsant effects by activating serotonergic neurons in genetically epilepsy-prone rats. *J. Pharmacol. Exp. Ther.*, 261: 652-659.

Yan QS, Yan SE. (2001). Activation of 5-HT(1B/1D) receptors in the mesolimbic dopamine system increases dopamine release from the nucleus accumbens: A icrodialysis study. *Eur. J. Pharmacol.*, 481: 05-64.

Yan QS. (2002). Reduced serotonin release and serotonin uptake sites in the rat nucleus accumbens and striatum after prenatal cocaine exposure. *Brain Res.*, 929: 59-69.

Yang CR, Mogenson GJ. (1990). Dopaminergic modulation of cholinergic responses in rat medial prefrontal cortex: an electrophysiological study. *Brain Res.*, 524: 271-281.

Yang CR, Seamans JK. (1996). Dopamine D1 receptor actions in layers of V-VI rat prefrontal cortex neurons in vitro: modulation of dendritic-somatic signal integration. *J. Neurosci.*, 16: 1922-1935.

Yeh GC, Bonhaus DW, Nadler JV, McNamara JO. (1989). N-methyl- D-aspartate receptor plasticity in kindling: quantitative and qualitative alterations in the N-methyl-D-aspartate receptor-channel complex. *Proc. Natl. Acad. Sci.*, 86: 8157-8160.

Yu L ,Nguyen H, Le H, Bloem LJ, Kozak CA, Hoffman BJ, Snutch TP, Lester HA, Davidson N, Luebbert H. (1991). The mouse 5-HT_{1C} receptor contains eight hydrophobic domains and is X-linked. *Mol. Brain Res.,* 11: 143-149.

Yu SP, Sensi SL, Canzoniero LM, Buisson A, Choi DW. (1997). Membrane-delimited modulation of NMDA currents by metabotropic glutamate receptor subtypes 1/5 in cultured mouse cortical neurons. *J. Physiol.*, 499: 721-732.

Zhang W, Linden DJ. (2006). Long-term depression at the mossy fiber in deep cerebellar nucleus synapse. *J. Neurosci.*, 26: 6935-6944.

Zifa E, Fillion G. (1992). 5-Hydroxytryptamine receptors. *Pharmacol. Rev.*, 44: 401-458.

www.ingramcontent.com/pod-product-compliance
Lightning Source LLC
Chambersburg PA
CBHW081213130726
47997CB00009B/2644